First World War
and Army of Occupation
War Diary
France, Belgium and Germany

4 DIVISION
11 Infantry Brigade
London Regiment
5th (City of London) Battalion (London Rifle Brigade)
4 November 1914 - 31 January 1916

WO95/1498/2

The Naval & Military Press Ltd
www.nmarchive.com
Published in association with The National Archives

Published by

The Naval & Military Press Ltd

Unit 10 Ridgewood Industrial Park,
Uckfield, East Sussex,
TN22 5QE England
Tel: +44 (0) 1825 749494

www.naval-military-press.com
www.nmarchive.com

This diary has been reprinted in facsimile from the original. Any imperfections are inevitably reproduced and the quality may fall short of modern type and cartographic standards.

Contents

Document type	Place/Title	Date From	Date To
Heading	1498/2 1 Battalion City of London L.R.B 1914 Nov 1916 Jan		
Heading	4 Division 11 Infy Bde 1-5th Battalion City Of London Regt. (L.R.B.) 1914 Nov-1916 Jan c		
Heading	4th Division 6th Infantry Bde 1/5th City Of London Regt. London Rifle Bde Joined Bde From U.K. 17-11-14 November & December 1914		
Miscellaneous	11th Brigade 4th Division. Disembarked Havre 5.11.14- Joined 11th Bde 17.11.14 1/5th City Of London Regiment (London Rifle Brigade) November 1914		
War Diary	Crow Borough	04/11/1914	04/11/1914
War Diary	Southampton	04/11/1914	04/11/1914
War Diary	Havre	05/11/1914	07/11/1914
War Diary	St Omer	08/11/1914	11/11/1914
War Diary	Wisques	12/11/1914	16/11/1914
War Diary	Haaze Brouck	17/11/1914	17/11/1914
War Diary	Baileul	18/11/1914	19/11/1914
War Diary	Romarin	20/11/1914	22/11/1914
War Diary	Ploegsteert	23/11/1914	30/11/1914
Miscellaneous	A Form Messages And Signals.		
Miscellaneous	C Form (Quadruplicate) Messages And Signals		
Miscellaneous	Appendix 3	18/11/1914	18/11/1914
Miscellaneous	A Form Messages And Signals		
Miscellaneous	C Form (Duplicate) Messages And Signals		
Heading	11th Brigade 4th Division 1/5th City of London Regiment (L.R.B.) December 1914		
War Diary	Ploegsteert	01/12/1914	31/12/1914
Miscellaneous	Special Order Of The Day By His Majesty The King Appendix VI	05/12/1914	05/12/1914
Miscellaneous	C Form (Duplicate) Messages And Signals		
Miscellaneous	A Form Messages And Signals		
Miscellaneous	Order Appendix IX	18/12/1914	18/12/1914
Miscellaneous	Messages And Signals App X		
Miscellaneous	C Form (Original) Messages And Signals		
Heading	4th Division 8th Infantry Bde 5th Battn London Regt. (L.R.B.) January To May 1915 To G.H.Q. 28-5-15		
Heading	4th Div. 11th Inf. Bde. War Diary 5th Battn. The London Regt. (L.R.B.) January 1915		
War Diary	Ploegsteert	01/01/1915	31/01/1915
Miscellaneous	Details Of Positions Of Coys		
Heading	4th Div. 11th Inf. Bde. War Diary 5th Battn. The London Regt. (L.R.B.) February 1915		
War Diary	Ploegsteert	01/02/1915	28/02/1915
Diagram etc	L.R.B. Trench		
Miscellaneous	Appendix XIII Method of Keeping Trench & C in State of Repair		
Heading	4th Div. 11th Inf. Bde. War Diary 5th Battn. The London Regt. (L.R.B.) March 1915		
War Diary	Ploegsteert	01/03/1915	20/03/1915
War Diary	Ploegsteert Wood	21/03/1915	31/03/1915

Miscellaneous	A Form Messages And Signals		
Miscellaneous	Battalion Order	20/03/1915	20/03/1915
Heading	4th Div. 11th Inf. Bde. War Diary 5th Battn. The London Regt. (L.R.B.) April 1915		
War Diary	Ploegsteert Wood	01/04/1915	23/04/1915
War Diary	Steenwerck	24/04/1915	24/04/1915
War Diary	Busseboom	25/04/1915	25/04/1915
War Diary	St. Jean	25/04/1915	30/04/1915
Miscellaneous	C Form (Original) Messages And Signals		
Operation(al) Order(s)	Operation Order No. 1 by Brig Genl J. Hasler Comdg 11 Inf Bde	24/04/1915	24/04/1915
Miscellaneous	Casualties		
Heading	4th Div 11th Inf. Bde. War Diary 5th Battn. The London Regt. (L.R.B.) May 1915 (to G.H.Q. 20.5.15.)		
War Diary	Trenches	01/05/1915	03/05/1915
War Diary	Elverdinghe	04/05/1915	04/05/1915
War Diary	In Wood	05/05/1915	19/05/1915
War Diary	Vlamertinghe	20/05/1915	20/05/1915
War Diary	Tatinghem	21/05/1915	31/05/1915
Miscellaneous	C Form (Duplicate) Messages And Signals		
Miscellaneous	C Form (Original) Messages And Signals		
Miscellaneous	A Form Messages And Signals		
Miscellaneous	C Form (Original) Messages And Signals		
Miscellaneous	The Officers Commanding 1st Bn London Rifle Brigade	19/05/1915	19/05/1915
Miscellaneous	Organisation of Composite Battn London Regiment Relief Of 6th Battn Welsh Regt. On Lines Of Communication	27/05/1915	27/05/1915
Miscellaneous	Organisation Composite Battalion London Regiment		
Miscellaneous	List Of Southern Railheads and Distribution of Troops on L. of 6		
Miscellaneous	Casualties	02/05/1915	02/05/1915
Heading	4th Division 1/5th London Regt (L.R.B.) Vol VIII 1-30.6.15		
War Diary	Tatinghem	01/06/1915	01/06/1915
War Diary	St. Omer	02/06/1915	30/06/1915
Miscellaneous	Copy of Letter from O.C. Queens Victoria's Rifles To O.C. London. Rifle Brigde		
Miscellaneous	Copy of Letter G.O.C. G.H.Q. Troops	05/06/1915	05/06/1915
Miscellaneous	Extract from Battalion Order	25/06/1915	25/06/1915
Miscellaneous	Copy of Extract From "The Lines" London Gazette. Honours.	24/06/1915	24/06/1915
Heading	4th Division 5th London (L.R. Bde) Vol IX 1-31-7-15		
War Diary	Camp St Omer	01/07/1915	31/07/1915
Heading	G.H.Q. 5th London (Rifles Bde) Rgt. Vol X From 1-31.8.15		
Heading	War Diary London Rifle Brigade 1st August 1915 To 31 August		
War Diary	Camp St Omer	01/08/1915	31/08/1915
Heading	War Diary of 1/5th London Regt (London Rifle Brigade) (1st Battalion) From 1st September 1915 To 30th September 1915 Vol XI		
War Diary	In Camp St. Omer	01/09/1915	30/09/1915
Miscellaneous	A Form Messages And Signals		
Miscellaneous	Routine Order By Colonel A, Sprat Commandent No 1 Sect S. Of C. September 30th 1915	30/09/1915	30/09/1915

Heading	War Diary of 1/5th Battalion City Of London (Rifles) (London Rifle Brigade) From 1st October 1915 To 31st October 1915 Vol XII		
War Diary	St. Omer	01/10/1915	02/10/1915
War Diary	Blendecques	03/10/1915	25/10/1915
War Diary	Ryfeld	26/10/1915	31/10/1915
Miscellaneous	Memorandum	01/10/1915	01/10/1915
Miscellaneous	O.B. 206. G.H.Q.T. 5876	14/10/1915	14/10/1915
Miscellaneous	Memorandum	19/10/1915	19/10/1915
Miscellaneous	O.C. London Rifle Brigade	22/10/1915	22/10/1915
Heading	1/5th London Nov. Vol XIII		
Heading	War Diary of 1/5th City Of London Rifles (London Rifles Brigade) From 1st November 1915 To 30th November 1915		
War Diary	Ryfeld	01/11/1915	23/11/1915
War Diary	Poperinghe	24/11/1915	28/11/1915
War Diary	Voormezeele	29/11/1915	30/11/1915
Operation(al) Order(s)	8th. Brigade Order No. 15	22/11/1915	22/11/1915
Miscellaneous	A Form Messages And Signals		
Operation(al) Order(s)	8th. Infantry Brigade Order No. 17	28/11/1915	28/11/1915
Heading	5th Battn City of London Rifles War Diary Dec 1915		
Heading	War Diary of 1/5th City Of London Rifles (London Rifles Brigade) From 1st December To 31st December 1916 Vol XIV		
War Diary	Voormezeele	01/12/1915	06/12/1915
War Diary	Poperinghe	07/12/1915	13/12/1915
War Diary	Voormezeele	14/12/1915	21/12/1915
War Diary	Poperinghe	22/12/1915	31/12/1915
Operation(al) Order(s)	8th. Infantry Brigade Order No. 18	05/12/1915	05/12/1915
Heading	8th Brigade 3rd Division War Diary Battalion Went to 56th Division (169th Bde) 5th February 1916 1/5th Battalion London Regiment January 1916		
Heading	3rd Div. 5th London Regt Jan Vol XV To 169 Bde 5/2/1916		
War Diary	Voormezeele	01/01/1916	04/01/1916
War Diary	Dickebusch	05/01/1916	10/01/1916
War Diary	Voormezeele	11/01/1916	18/01/1916
War Diary	Reninghelst	19/01/1916	25/01/1916
War Diary	Voormezeele	26/01/1916	31/01/1916

1498/2

1 Battalion City of London.

LRB.

– 1914 Nov –

1916 Jan

+ ~~3RD~~ DIVISION

11 ~~8TH~~ INFY BDE

1-5TH BATTALION

CITY OF LONDON ~~RIFLES~~ REGT. (L.R.B.)

~~OCT-DEC 1915.~~

1914 NOV – 1916 JAN

FROM UK

To 56 DIV 169 BDE FEB 1916

ATTACHED TO G H Q TROOPS

1915 MAY – 1915 SEPT

BOX 1498

~~4th~~ 6 Division

6 ~~4th~~ Infantry Bde

1/5th City of London Regt
London Rifle Bde

L. R. B

Joined Bde from U.K. 17-11-14

November + December
1914

11th Brigade.

4th Division.

Disembarked HAVRE 5.11.14 - Joined 11th Bde 17.11.14

1/5th CITY OF LONDON REGIMENT

(London Rifle Brigade)

NOVEMBER 1 9 1 4

Instructions regarding War Diaries and Intelligence Summaries are contained in F. S. Regs., Part II. and the Staff Manual respectively. Title pages will be prepared in manuscript.

WAR DIARY
or
~~INTELLIGENCE SUMMARY~~

(Erase heading not required.)

Army Form C. 2118.

Hour, Date, Place			Summary of Events and Information	Remarks and references to Appendices
11.35am / 1.5 p.M.	4.11.14	Crowborough	Left in 2 Detachments for Southampton	AWr
		Southampton	Embarked on S.S CHYEBASSA. Fine weather	
5 p.m	"		received secret orders Cypher code. Strength 863 men including attached 29 officers 1 M.O.	
		HAVRE	. arrived weather fine	AWr
11 a.m.	5.11.14		Disembarked	
12.30 pM	"	"	Arrived Rest camp	
2.30 pm	"	"		
11 a.m.	6.11.14	"	received orders to entrain at GARES DES MARCHANDISES at 4.30 p.m	AWr
9 p.m.	"	"	Left by train. Received B[3] Ordre de Transport. weather fine	
	7.11.14		Route via ROUEN, ABANCOURT, AUMALE, ABBEVILLE	
			Fine but misty	
			Told we are to go to ST. OMER	
5.30	"		Arrive ST. OMER	AWr
7.30	"		Disentrained and went into barracks quite close for night	
			Received secret tactical orders from experience gained in war.	
			Allotted to Army Troops which are formed into a Reserve Brigade	
			under Col. CHICHESTER	
1.30 p.m.	8.11.14	St. OMER	Left for BENEDICTINE MONASTERY, WISQUES 3½ miles W by S of ST. OMER – fine	AWr
9.a.m – 4.30 p.M.	9.11.14	"	Battalion training in attack	
7am – 5p.m	10.11.14		Digging on the BLONDEQUES – AIRE position – rainy	
8 am – 4.30pm	11.11.14		C-in-C visited billets in morning	AWr
			Inspected by Brigadier in attack – Brigade MAJOR – MAJOR NEEDHAM	

Instructions regarding War Diaries and Intelligence Summaries are contained in F. S. Regs., Part II. and the Staff Manual respectively. Title pages will be prepared in manuscript.

WAR DIARY
or
INTELLIGENCE SUMMARY
(Erase heading not required.)

Army Form C. 2118.

Hour, Date, Place	Summary of Events and Information	Remarks and references to Appendices
8.30 a.m. – 4.30 p.m. – 12.11.14 ~~St. OMER~~ WISQUES	Musketry on ranges to try new rifles at St. OMER	Aws
7.15 a.m. – 2 p.m. – 13.11.14 WISQUES	Told next to go to front. Digging on the AIRE–HELTAUT position. Very wet all day	Aws
2 p.m. – 7 p.m. 14.11.14 WISQUES	Battn training in attack & night digging – cold & unsettled	Aws
2 p.m. – 5 p.m. 15.11.14 WISQUES	Route march – rain & cold. Received marching order at 5 p.m. to join 11th Inf. Bde	Appendix I
8 a.m. – 2.45 p.m. 16.11.14 WISQUES	Marched to HAAZEBROUCK – 17 miles – 15 sick to hospital (clearing) at BLANDEQUES	Aws
8 a.m. – 11.45 p.m. 17.11.14 HAAZEBROUCK	Marched to BAILEUL – 11 miles – reported Hqrs 3rd Corps at BAILEUL ordered to Billets. Reported to Hqrs 4th Div at NIEPPE and to Hqrs 11th Bde at PLOEGSTEERT	Aws
7.30 p.m.	Received order to remain in Billets – Wet	Appen. II
18.11.14. BAILEUL	Billets – very cold.	Aws

S. J. R. B.

Army Form C. 2118.

Instructions regarding War Diaries and Intelligence Summaries are contained in F. S. Regs., Part II. and the Staff Manual respectively. Title pages will be prepared in manuscript.

WAR DIARY
or
INTELLIGENCE SUMMARY
(Erase heading not required.)

Hour, Date, Place	Summary of Events and Information	Remarks and references to Appendices
10 a.m. 19.11.14 BAILEUL 12 noon	Marched for ROMARIN arrived " in Billets to join 11th Inf Bde commanded by Brig Gen HUNTER WESTON - Showed -	Appendix III & IV
3.45 p.m. 20/11/14 ROMARIN	Eight ½ Coys of A, B, D, E, G, H, O, P, Q proceeded to trenches to take place of 4 platoons of S.L.I and 4 platoons of HANTS REGT. on E edge of PLOEGSTEERT WOOD. These to be mixed up with the regulars and not to go in as single ½ Coys - Very fine and freezing all day.	
21/11/14 ROMARIN	4 platoons of HANTS & 4 platoons of S.L.I came last night to live in our Billets whilst our men are in the trenches. Freezing & v. fine	

Instructions regarding War Diaries and Intelligence Summaries are contained in F. S. Regs., Part II. and the Staff Manual respectively. Title pages will be prepared in manuscript.

WAR DIARY
or
INTELLIGENCE SUMMARY
(Erase heading not required.)

Army Form C. 2118.

Hour, Date, Place	Summary of Events and Information	Remarks and references to Appendices
2.30 p.m 22/11/14 ROMARIN	½ Bn left for billets in PLOEGSTEERT 3 miles away E.	
3.0 p.m " "	" " " " " 600 N. of " on MESSINES ROAD at Farm where the report centre of the 11th Inf. Bde is. Fine and frosty.	App. V
23/11/14 PLOESTEERT	Coys patrolled wood to make themselves acquainted with paths to various trenches. i.e. Battns holding E front of wood from N to S in order named 1st S.L.I. 1st R.B. 1st HANTS. 1st E.LANCS. L.R.B in reserve (in centre of W edge of wood) - Freezing - Sent up remaining ½ Coys of Battn to trenches i.e. 2 half Coys to each Battn.	No. 81 : Pte Dunnett (killed) 1st casualty " 786 " Herman (slightly wounded)
24/11/14 "	Started 4 Coy. Organization	
25/11/14 "	All day working parties - warmer and general thaw	
26th "	8 platoons attached as units to battns of Brigade - 2 to each Bn in trenches Working parties in wood. 2 men slightly wounded	2 slightly wounded
27/11/14 "	Much warmer but ground & roads in very muddy condition. Working parties in wood. Receive news of RUSSIAN victory at LODZ. W O asks for opinion of 4 versus 8 Coy organization having regard to experience of war. Answered that 4 Coy was the only expedient as the difficulty of adhering to 8 Coys with 4 Coys in the Regulars outweighed all other disadvantages such as lack of experience of officers.	1 slightly wounded

Instructions regarding War Diaries and Intelligence Summaries are contained in F. S. Regs., Part II. and the Staff Manual respectively. Title pages will be prepared in manuscript.

WAR DIARY
or
INTELLIGENCE SUMMARY
(Erase heading not required.)

Army Form C. 2118.

Hour, Date, Place		Summary of Events and Information	Remarks and references to Appendices	
28.11.14	PLOEGSTEERT	Working parties in wood all day – 4 platoons night digging with R.B.	1/Pte Pile (Killed) 2 slightly wounded	AW
29.11.14	"	" " " " " " " "		AW
		8 platoons came out of trenches. No 4 Coy. proceeded to ROMARIN in billets		
30.11.14	"	Rest for Battn to reorganise and wash.		AW

"A" Form. Army Form C. 2121.

MESSAGES AND SIGNALS. No. of Message 360

Prefix OB Code CC m. Words 79 Charge

Office of Origin and Service Instructions. GHQ Priority

Sent At m. To By

PRIORITY
O.B. General Staff.

(Signature of "Franking Officer.")

ARMY TELEGRAPHS 6 Date 15.XI.14. HQ From

TO 5th London Regt WISQUES
~~3rd Corps~~
~~2nd Corps~~
Appendix I

Sender's Number	Day of Month	In reply to Number	AAA
* AT 315	15		

march	tomorrow	to	HAZEBROUCK	where
you	will	halt	for	the
night	aaa	Following	day	to
PLOEGSTREET		East	of	BAILLEUL
where	you	form	11th	Infantry
Bde	aaa	Send	on	officers
on	~~[illegible]~~ first	day	~~to~~	report
		2nd	Corps	HAZE-
-BROUCK	for	orders	as	regards
billets	and	on	second	day
to	HQ	3rd	Corps	BAILLEUL
as	regards	your	movements	
East	of	BAILLEUL	aaa	addressed
London	Regt	repeated	3rd	and
2nd	Corps			

From GHQ
Place
Time 3.5 pm

The above may be forwarded as now corrected. (Z) C Harington, maj

Censor. Signature of Addressor or person authorised to telegraph in his name

*This line should be erased if not required.

2051 M. & Co. Ltd. Wt. W929/549—100,000. 6/14. Forms C2121/10.

"C" Form (Quadruplicate). Army Form C. 2123 A.

MESSAGES AND SIGNALS. No. of Message..........

Sm E&R 64

Appendix II

Charges to Pay: YD Phillips

Office Stamp: 3RD A. H. Q. 17 NOV. 14 6p

Service Instructions. One of 2 adds.

Handed in at the YD Office, at 5.26p m. Received here at 6p m

TO London Rifle Brigade

Appendix II

Sender's Number	Day of Month.	In reply to Number.	AAA
GG12	17th		

No accommodation for London Rifle Bde until morning 19th aaa Please keep this battalion at BAILLEUL till then aaa It should then proceed to ROMARIN under instructions which will be issued direct aaa Supply vehicles should draw supplies tomorrow from 4th Div TRAIN at STEENWERCK aaa Addressed 3rd Corps Repeated London R B

FROM Fourth Divn

PLACE

TIME 5.45pm

GALE & POLDEN, LTD. PRINTERS, ALDERSHOT.
(69,017). Wt. 7981—443. 40,000 Pads. 4/13. W.

Somersets
E. Lanc.
Hants
Rif Brig.
S10.5/ London Rif. Brig.

Appendix 3

The Maj. Gen Condy. wishes it to be clearly understood throughout his Brigade that the business of Officers and N.C.O's is to direct the action of their unit or sub-unit; & that it is wrong for a Commander to relinquish this; his proper duty, in order to attend to a wounded man.

18-11-14. W.H.M. Freeston Capt
Staff Capt 11th Inf. Bde.

"A" Form. Army Form C. 2121.

MESSAGES AND SIGNALS.

No. of Message........

Prefix........ Code........ m. | Words | Charge

Office of Origin and Service Instructions.

Sent
At........ m.
To........
By........

This message is on a/c of:
.... *Service.*
(Signature of "Franking Officer.")

Recd. at........ m.
Date........
From........
By........

Appendix IV

TO { Somersets – Hants

Sender's Number	Day of Month	In reply to Number	AAA
* BM 22	Nineteenth		

I have decided to send four platoons of the London Rifle Brigade to you tomorrow afternoon AAA One platoon to be absorbed by each of your four Coys AAA One Captain and four subalterns will be sent to you AAA subalterns should act as assistants to four good platoon commanders, the Captain as assistant to a good Coy Commander AAA I will let you know exact strengths later so that you may send back equivalent numbers to L.R.B. AAA One guide from each of your Coys should be at Brigade H.Q. by 1.30 pm tomorrow –

2

London Rifle Brigade

Above for your information – Please let me know exact numbers.

From ~~Eleventh Inf Brig [illegible]~~
Place
Time 5.45 pm.

The above may be forwarded as now corrected. (Z) A. J. Ross BM.

Censor. Signature of Addressor or person authorised to telegraph in his name.

* This line should be erased if not required.

"C" Form (Duplicate). Army Form C. 2123.

MESSAGES AND SIGNALS. No. of Message

ZK

	Charges to Pay. £ s. d.	Office Stamp. EX 22.11.14

Service Instructions. Three addresses

Handed in at the 11th Brig Office, at 9-59p.m. Received here at 10-20p.m.

TO REPORT CENTRE E. LAN. LONDON RIF BRIG

Sender's Number.	Day of Month.	In reply to Number.	AAA
BM18	22nd		

Please send out scouts towards LE BIZET to look for a platoon of 2ND MONMOUTH REGT. who are supposed to have started from LE-BIZET at 2pm today to go as a working party to ESSEX REGT. who are one mile south of LEGHEER aaa The platoon is missing AAA Report to Brig Hdqrs

FROM ELEVENTH INF BRIG

PLACE

TIME 9-59 pm

W. 5376—433. 75,000 Pads—12/12—B. & F.—Forms/C.2123/1.

11th Brigade.

4th Division.

1/5th CITY OF LONDON REGIMENT (L.R.B.)

DECEMBER 1 9 1 4.

Instructions regarding War Diaries and Intelligence Summaries are contained in F. S. Regs., Part II. and the Staff Manual respectively. Title pages will be prepared in manuscript.

WAR DIARY
or
~~INTELLIGENCE SUMMARY.~~
(*Erase heading not required.*)

Army Form C. 2118.

L R B

Hour, Date, Place	Summary of Events and Information	Remarks and references to Appendices
1/12/14 PLOEGSTEERT	Rest day for washing – No 4 Coy to ROMARIN in billets	[illegible]
2/12/14 "	Sent up 8 platoons in evening to trenches, two to each battn of brigade. Received telegram from Bde to send a representation to be inspected by the King at NIEPPE.	One wounded
8.30–4pm 3/12/14 "	Working parties in wood. 2 platoons from No 4 Coy represented the Bn at NIEPPE under Capt MACGEAGH for inspection by the King. All our guns W of us opened very heavy & rapid fire from 2pm–2.20pm	Heard afterwards this was for the King's benefit. No 5 Pte PEARSE C.N. died of wounds and buried at BAILLEUL No 9932 Pte PROTHEROE A. [illegible]
8 a.m. 4/12/14 "	Capture of DE WET and his commando confirmed by message from 11th Bde	
8.30 a.m – 4.30 pm "	Working parties in wood.	5 men wounded by shell. (No 3 Coy)
8.30 a.m – 4.30 p.m 5/12/14 "	Working parties in wood. No 4 Coy and No 3 Coy exchange billets 8 Platoons come out of trenches. Whole Battn in billets here ~~except~~ ~~No 3 Coy at ROMARIN.~~ No 3 Coy taking over E. LANCS reserve billets.	1 man wounded (No 4 Coy)

(73989) W4141—463. 400,000. 9/14. H.&J.Ltd. Forms/C. 2118/10.

Army Form C. 2118.

Instructions regarding War Diaries and Intelligence Summaries are contained in F. S. Regs., Part II. and the Staff Manual respectively. Title pages will be prepared in manuscript.

WAR DIARY
or
~~INTELLIGENCE~~ SUMMARY

(Erase heading not required.)

L.R.B.

Hour, Date, Place	Summary of Events and Information	Remarks and references to Appendices
8·30 a.m. - 4 pm. 6/12/14 PLOEGSTEERT	Working Parties in Wood. ~~See~~	See Appx. VI
8·30 a.m. - 4 pm 7/12/14 "	" " " " also route march by Coys.	
8 pm - 4 a.m	" " " " (Hants Area)	
9 a.m - 12·30 pm. 8/12/14 "	" " " " Battn goes into trenches - each Coy attached to other regular battns of Brigade.	Pte Sutton No 37 killed; " WARD E.J. No 62 killed; 2 wounded. No 469 Pte THORNTON E.C. killed; 1 wounded
9/12/14		
10/12/14		3 wounded; LT. KIRBY A. slightly wounded; No 9838 Pte Potts killed; No 140 Pte BRADLEY [illegible] at BAILEUL

Instructions regarding War Diaries and Intelligence Summaries are contained in F. S. Regs., Part II. and the Staff Manual respectively. Title pages will be prepared in manuscript.

WAR DIARY
or
~~INTELLIGENCE SUMMARY~~
(Erase heading not required.)

Army Form C. 2118.

Hour, Date, Place	Summary of Events and Information	Remarks and references to Appendices
~~8.30 – 4 pm~~ ans 11/12/14 PLOEGSTREET	~~Working parties in wood~~ ans. Coys come out of trenches except No 3 and form Bn Reserve in PLOEGSTREET	{Sgt No 8050 WARNER killed {1 wounded [illegible] Capt & Adj
8.30–4 p.m. 12/12/14 "	Working parties in wood. (Orders to go to NIEPPE to rest & wash. No 3 Coy joins Reserve. cancelled. Billets changed to S. of village near BREWERY, PLOEGSTREET. Bn HQrs at ESTAMINET, next to BREWERY]	
9 a.m. – 4 p.m. 13/12/14 "	Working parties in wood. Several guns come up to this part of the line. Weather has been very wet all this week and trenches terribly bad. Hear there is to be an attack somewhere between Coast and ARMENTIERES (unofficial)	{No 2980 Daphne killed {3 | [illegible] Billett wounded { | 2 wounded See Append. VII
14.12.14 "	Shelling by our guns intermittently all day	L.R.B.

/ 2

Instructions regarding War Diaries and Intelligence Summaries are contained in F. S. Regs., Part II. and the Staff Manual respectively. Title pages will be prepared in manuscript.

WAR DIARY
or
~~INTELLIGENCE~~ SUMMARY
(Erase heading not required.)

Army Form C. 2118.

Hour, Date, Place	Summary of Events and Information	Remarks and references to Appendices
9a.m.-4p.m. 15/12/14 PLOEGSTREET	Working parties in wood. Fine. Heavy shelling by our guns.	6 men wounded
" " 16/12/14 "	" " " Wet " " " "	
9a.m - 3a.m 17/12/14 "	" " " " " " " "	
9a.m - 3a.m 18/12/14 "	" " " " " " " "	Appen VIII, " IX
	11th Inf Bde to attack - L.R.B. as Bde reserve. &c	
1 p.m. 19/12/14 "	In position. V. Heavy shelling by our guns all morning.	No 9209 L/cpl Roache killed, 2 men wounded
7.30 p.m. "	Ordered to take up line of breastworks No 1 - 26.	
	Objective not attained - some houses and 1 line of trenches captured.	
	In reserve trenches.	
7.30 a.m. 20/12/14	Returned to Billets	
12.30 p.m. "	Received congratulatory message to Brigade from G.O.C.	App. X
9 P.M. "		

L.R.B.

1247 W 3299 200,000 (E) 8/14 J.B.C. & A. Forms/C. 2118/11.

Instructions regarding War Diaries and Intelligence Summaries are contained in F. S. Regs., Part II. and the Staff Manual respectively. Title pages will be prepared in manuscript.

WAR DIARY
or
INTELLIGENCE SUMMARY
(Erase heading not required.)

Army Form C. 2118.

Hour, Date, Place	Summary of Events and Information	Remarks and references to Appendices
21/12/14 PLOEGSTEERT	Working parties	[illegible]
8am – 1pm 22/12/14 "	Bathing at NIEPPE by coys and return to billets same day	
23/12/14 "	A coy. attached to each Batt. of the Brigade from to-night in trenches. Batt. H^d Q^rs changed to their original place. C.O. in cmd of reserve coys in billets.	
24/12/14 "	King & Queen's Xmas card issued. Fine.	~~L/Cpl~~ P^te 9230 BASSINGHAM A.R. Killed.
25/12/14	Freezing – very quiet day practically no shooting	J. R. B

(E) 8/14 J.B.C. & A. Forms/C. 2118/11.

Instructions regarding War Diaries and Intelligence Summaries are contained in F.S. Regs., Part II. and the Staff Manual respectively. Title pages will be prepared in manuscript.

WAR DIARY
or
INTELLIGENCE SUMMARY.
(Erase heading not required.)

Army Form C. 2118.

Hour, Date, Place		Summary of Events and Information	Remarks and references to Appendices
26.12.14	PLOEGSTEERT	Freezing & snowing – very quiet day.	
27.12.14	"	V. cold " " " C.O. goes on 10 days leave	
		Owing to shortage of officers in SOMERSETS the following officers of L.R.B lent to them under arrangements with G.O.C. :-	
		Capts. THOMPSON and Somers-Smith Lieuts CHOLMELEY, FURSDON, CARTWRIGHT }	
28.12.14	"	V. bad storm in evening. O.C. L.R.B now in cmd of only 2 Reserve Coys. in billets, remainder under O.C. units concerned.	
29.12.14	"	Quiet day & v. little sniping	
30.12.14	"	" " " " " "	
31.12.14	"	" " " " "	

(73989) W4141—463. 400,000. 9/14. H.&J.Ltd. Forms/C. 2118/10.

Appendix VI

Special Order of the Day

BY

HIS MAJESTY THE KING.

Officers, Non-commissioned Officers and Men,—

I am very glad to have been able to see my Army in the Field.

I much wished to do so in order to gain a slight experience of the life you are leading.

I wish I could have spoken to you all, to express my admiration of the splendid manner in which you have fought and are still fighting against a powerful and relentless enemy.

By your discipline, pluck and endurance, inspired by the indomitable regimental spirit, you have not only upheld the tradition of the British Army but added fresh lustre to its history.

I was particularly impressed by your soldierly, healthy, cheerful appearance.

I cannot share in your trials, dangers and successes; but I can assure you of the proud confidence and gratitude of myself and of your fellow countrymen.

We follow you in our daily thoughts on your certain road to victory.

GEORGE, R.I.

General Headquarters,

December 5th, 1914.

1st Printing Co., R.E. G.H.Q. 309.

"C" Form (Duplicate). Army Form C. 2123.

MESSAGES AND SIGNALS. No. of Message 4

Charges to Pay. £ s. d.	Office Stamp.
	LRB 14/12/14.

2 K

Service Instructions. Four addresses

Handed in at .... Office ...... m. Received 9.30 a.m.

TO SOM. L.I. E. LANCS. HANTS RIF. BDE L.R.B.

Sender's Number	Day of Month	In reply to Number	AAA
BM 5	14th		

At	about	11	a.m.	and
3	p.m.	today	there	will
be	bursts	of	rifle	and
artillery	fire	along	the	front
held	by	~~S~~	the	12th
INF	BDE			

APPENDIX VII

FROM 11th INF BDE

PLACE & TIME 9.14 a.m.

W.2384—583. 30,000 Pads—8/14. S. B. Ltd.—Forms/C.2123.

"A" Form. Army Form C. 2121.

MESSAGES AND SIGNALS.

No. of Message

Prefix ____ Code ____ m. Office of Origin and Service Instructions.	Words / Charge	This message is on a/c of: APP VIII Service. (Signature of "Franking Officer.")	Recd. at ____ m. Date From By
	Sent At ____ m. To By		

TO				
	SOM. L. I.	E. LANCS.	HANTS.	RIF BRIG
	MOUNTAIN BTY	M. Co R.E.		

Sender's Number	Day of Month	In reply to Number	AAA
* B.M. 16	18th.		

(1) Ref	sketch	map	PLOEGSTEERT	WOOD
and	sheet 28 S.W.	The	11th INF	BRIG will
attack	to-morrow	and	capture	the
bight	in	their	line	AAA
The	12th	BRIGADE	on	our
right	and	10th BRIG	on	our
left	have	been	ordered	to
do	all	in	their	power
to	assist	our	brigade	AAA
The	Div	ARTY	has	been
ordered	to	heavily	shell	the
enemy's	position	till	the	moment
of	attack	when	they	will
lengthen	their	range	AAA.	The
advance	will	commence	from	the
edge	of	the	wood	exactly
at	2.30 p.m	to-morrow,	watches	being

From

Place

Time

The above may be forwarded as now corrected. (Z)

Censor. Signature of Addressor or person authorised to telegraph in his name

*This line should be erased if not required

662 M. & Co. Ltd Wt W929/549–100,000. 6/14. Forms C2121/10.

"A" Form. Army Form C. 2121.

MESSAGES AND SIGNALS.

No. of Message

Prefix ____ Code ____ m.	Words	Charge	This message is on a/c of:	Recd. at ____ m.
Office of Origin and Service Instructions.	Sent		____ Service.	Date
	At ____ m.			From
	To			By
	By		(Signature of "Franking Officer.")	

TO (2)

* Sender's Number	Day of Month	In reply to Number	AAA

not	by	BRIG	HQRS	through
telephone	offices	at	10 a.m.	to-morrow
AAA				
(2) The	RIF	BRIG	will	attack
astride	the	road	running	E
by	N	from	GERMAN	HOUSE
Objective	the	enemy's	defences	about
300	yards	E	of	GERMAN
HOUSE	10	Sappers	CoRE	are
allotted	to	1st	RIF	BRIG
(3) The	SOMERSETS	will	attack	on
[illegible]	left	of	the	RIF
BRIG	their	objective	being	the
enemy's	breastworks	in	their	front.
They	will	be	assisted	by
flanking	fire	from	their	men
holding	their	left	trenches	and

From

Place

Time

The above may be forwarded as now corrected. (Z)

Censor. Signature of Addressor or person authorised to telegraph in his name

*This line should be erased if not required

2662 M. & Co. Ltd Wt W929/549—100,000. 6/14. Forms C2121/10.

"A" Form. Army Form C. 2121.

MESSAGES AND SIGNALS. No. of Message

Prefix Code m. | Words | Charge | This message is on a/c of: | Recd. at m.

Office of Origin and Service Instructions. | Sent At m. To By | Service. (Signature of "Franking Officer.") | Date From By

TO (3)

Sender's Number | Day of Month | In reply to Number | AAA

from their battalion machine guns.
6 Sappers) Co R.E are allotted to
Som L.I.
(4) The HANTS will co-operate with
the attack of the RIF BRIG by
keeping down the enemy's fire
to their front The HANTS
will also come up on
the right of the RIF
BRIG and fill in the
gap at the Northern end
of the HANTS trench
(5) The E. LANCS will assist the
attack by keeping down the
enemy's fire to their front.
Their machine guns will fire
on the ground E of the height.

From

Place

Time

The above may be forwarded as now corrected. (Z)

Censor. Signature of Addressor or person authorised to telegraph in his name

*This line should be erased if not required.

M. & Co. Ltd. Wt. W929/519—100,000. 6/14. Forms C2121/10.

"A" Form.

Army Form C. 2121.

MESSAGES AND SIGNALS.

No. of Message

Prefix / Code m.	Words	Charge	This message is on a/c of:	Recd. at m.
Office of Origin and Service Instructions.	Sent		Service.	Date
	At m.			From
	To			
	By		(Signature of "Franking Officer.")	By

TO (4)

Sender's Number	Day of Month	In reply to Number	AAA
*			

(6) BRIGADE RESERVE:- LONDON R.B.
HQRS:- house on the MESSINES-PLOEGSTEERT road S.E. of the Report Centre. One Company farm 300 yards West of the Report Centre - One Company North end of PLOEGSTEERT 2 companies BUNTER AVENUE.

(7) BRIGADE Ammunition Reserve on the PLOEGSTEERT road S.E. of the Report Centre

(8) Three Rach ARTILLERY guns will support the attack the 2 guns in PLOEGSTEERT WOOD opening fire at 2p.m. and ceasing at 2.20p.m precisely. The Northern Gun will be prepared to move forward behind the RIF BRIG to blow down any houses

From

Place

Time

The above may be forwarded as now corrected. (Z)

Censor. Signature of Addressor or person authorised to telegraph in his name

*This line should be erased if not required

3662 M. & Co. Ltd. Wt W928/549—100,000. 6/14. Forms C2121/10.

"A" Form. Army Form C. 2121.

MESSAGES AND SIGNALS.

No. of Message ______

Prefix ______ Code ______ m. Office of Origin and Service Instructions.	Words	Charge	This message is on a/c of: ______ Service. (Signature of "Franking Officer.")	Recd. at ______ m.
	Sent			Date ______
	At ______ m.			From ______
	To ______			
	By ______			By ______

TO (5)

Sender's Number	Day of Month	In reply to Number	AAA
*			

held	by	the	enemy	The
gun	South	of	the	EAST
LANCS	HDQRS	will	open	fire
at	9 a.m.	with	the	remainder
of	the	Artillery	and	continue
firing	throughout	the	day	at
objectives	separately	detailed		
(9) The	Div	Machine	Guns	have
been	ordered	for	to	assist
the	attack	and	four	will
co-operate	from	the	eastern	Ledge
of	PLOEGSTEERT	WOOD.		
(10) The	21	sections	RE	detailed
to	assist	the	Eleventh	Brig
will	be	disposed	as	follows
16	men	with	first	line
troops	as	above	with	crowbars

From
Place
Time

The above may be forwarded as now corrected. (Z)

Censor. Signature of Addressor or person authorised to telegraph in his name

*This line should be erased if not required

3662 M. & Co. Ltd. Wt W929/549 -100,000. 6/14. Forms C2121/10.

"A" Form.

Army Form C. 2121.

MESSAGES AND SIGNALS.

No. of Message

Prefix Code m. | Words | Charge

Office of Origin and Service Instructions.

Sent At m. To By

This message is on a/c of: Service.

(Signature of "Franking Officer.")

Recd. at m. Date From By

TO

6

Sender's Number | Day of Month | In reply to Number | AAA

hand grenades etc. to break any houses which may be found to be occupied by Germans. 2nd party will material for making good the defences gained, will come forward with the supporting line. Third party will make good the communications as soon as the objective is attained.

(11) Ammunition 200 rounds per man

(12) Food:- Iron rations & one days preserved ration

(13) Greatcoats & Packs will NOT be worn.

(14) Reports to the Report Centre

Acknowledge

From Eleventh Brig

Place

Time 5-53 P.M

The above may be forwarded as now corrected.

Censor.

(Z) G. T. Boyd Capt 11th Brig

Signature of Addressor or person authorised to telegraph in his name

*This line should be erased if not required

3662 M. & Co. Ltd Wt W929/519-100,000. 6/14. Forms C2121/10.

Orders by LT COL EARL CAIRNS
Cmdg LRB
18/12/14

Appendix IX

Ref. sketch map PLOEGSTREET WOOD and sheet 28 S.W.

The 11th INF. BDE will attack and capture the tight in their line assisted by 10th and 12th Bn

The Battn will be in reserve as follows:—

No 1 Coy in S end of BUNTER AVENUE
Coy. H.Q.s on S. Corduroy Path

No 3 — on left of No 1 Coy
Coy. H.Q.s on N Corduroy Path

No 2 Coy in houses at end of MESSINES – PLOEGSTREET road 400 yds N of CHURCH

No 4 Coy in farm 300 yards behind

REPORT CENTRE

Batt^n HQrs same as before ~~[illegible]~~

moving into present billets (a house on the road S.E. of REPORT CENTRE)

M.O. in house next door to Batt^n HQrs.

M.G. detachment to be with No 2 Coy

All Coys to be in position detailed above by 1 p.m.

Batt^n to move from billets by Coys starting at 11.45 a.m. at 1/4 of an hour interval in following order

No 3 No 1 No 4 No 2

Ordinary precautions against enemy artillery being taken

Besides the iron ration and unexpended portion of the days ration an extra days ration will be carried

62

2 cooks per Coy will remain [illegible]
tea' will be left HQRS
Battn Scouts and Coy. representatives will
be at Battn HQRS
2[illegible] rounds S A A to be carried
The Bn S.A.A. dump on the PLOEGSTEERT
road S E of REPORT CENTRE

[illegible signature] Capt & Adj.

7.30 pm

(Original). Army Form C. 2123.

MESSAGES AND SIGNALS.

No. of Message

Prefix Code Words | Received | Sent, or sent out | Office Stamp.

£ s. d.

Charges to collect

From

By

At m.

To APP

By

×

Service Instructions.

5 [illegible]

Handed in at Office m. Received m.

TO SOM L I ESSEX HANTS
RIF BRG L R B

*Sender's Number	Day of Month	In reply to Number	AAA
BM 47	20th		

The	G	O	C	[illegible]
	Corps	and	4th	DIV
has	been	personally	to see	the
Brigadier	and	has	asked	to
convey	to	the	officers	and men
of	the	11th	INF	BDE
engaged	in	yesterday's	attack	their
sincere	appreciation	of	the	performance
and	gallantry	under	most	trying
circumstances	AAA	The	Brigadier	has
already	expressed	his	commendation	of
	conduct	of	the	Brigade
in	the	message	he	sent
at	the	conclusion	of	the
operations	and	in	his	personal
visit	to	the	battalions	concerned
in	PLOEGSTEERT	WOOD		last

FROM

PLACE & TIME

* This line should be erased if not required.

W.2384—583. 30,000 Pads—8/14. S. B. Ltd.—Forms/C.2123.

"C" Form (Original). Army Form C. 2123.

MESSAGES AND SIGNALS. No. of Message

Prefix ... Code ... Words ...	Received	Sent, or sent out	Office Stamp.
£ s. d. Charges to collect	From ... By ...	At ... m. To ... By ...	
Service Instructions.			

Handed in at ... Office ... m. Received ... m.

TO

*Sender's Number	Day of Month	In reply to Number	AAA

[illegible]ght AAA The object of the
operation was to [illegible] the
enemy to their ground by
the fear of our attack
and so to prevent him
moving troops against the RUSSIANS
AAA This object has been
attained and incidentally we have
gained ground the edge of
the wood and the house
which was troublesome to us as
giving shelter to snipers AAA
The 11th [illegible] BN has always done well
and has done well again

FROM
PLACE & TIME Gen Hunter-Weston
6 pm

* This line should be erased if not required.

W.2384—586. 80,000 Pads—8/14. S. B. Ltd.—Forms/C.2123.

1

~~6~~ 4
~~1~~th Division

8 ~~11th~~ Infantry Bde

5th Battn London Regt (L.R.B.)

January to May 1915

To G.H.Q. 28-5-15

4th Div.
11th Inf. Bde.

WAR DIARY

5TH BATTN. THE LONDON REGT. (L.R.B.)

J A N U A R Y

1 9 1 5.

Instructions regarding War Diaries and Intelligence Summaries are contained in F. S. Regs., Part II. and the Staff Manual respectively. Title pages will be prepared in manuscript.

WAR DIARY
or
~~INTELLIGENCE~~ SUMMARY
(~~Erase heading not required.~~)

Army Form C. 2118.

Hour, Date, Place		Summary of Events and Information	Remarks and references to Appendices
1.1.15	PLOEGSTEERT	Quiet day	Any.
2.1.15	"	Received order from 2nd Army to the effect that "informal truce with the Enemy was to cease and any officer or NCO found having initiated one would be tried by C.M."	2 wounded
3.1.15	"	Usual sniping and intermittent shelling Rain	2nd LIEUT. WITT W.L. 2 Coy.
4.1.15	"	All Coys called back to billets to take up new line of trenches. BREWERY Billets reoccupied	No 8929 Pte JENKIN T.H. 1 Coy. " 9391 Pte PECK R.E. 4 Coy. (Names sent up for good work.)
5.1.15		In Billets. Allotted line from WARNAVE River to ESTAMINET now held by ESSEX REGT of 12th Brigade	Pte 9620 CORBLE E. Killed
6.1.15		In Billets. Col. 2d Cairnes returns from leave.	
7.1.15		Trenches to be held by Battn decreased Following line to be taken over from to-night. From WARNAVE River to a point about 280 S in prolongation of E. LANES on N. By 1 Coy. ESSEX 12th Bde prolonging line to S. Supporting Coy in farm 300 NE of BREWERY with 1 platoon in farm houses about 800 yds W of front trenches. Farms to be put in a state of defence.	

Instructions regarding War Diaries and Intelligence Summaries are contained in F. S. Regs., Part II. and the Staff Manual respectively. Title pages will be prepared in manuscript.

WAR DIARY
or
INTELLIGENCE SUMMARY
(Erase heading not required.)

Army Form C. 2118.

Hour, Date, Place	Summary of Events and Information	Remarks and references to Appendices
7.1.15 (Cont) PLOEGSTEERT	Mountain gun near this farm. Reserve Coy at 11th Brigade Reserve in PLOEGSTEERT. 1 Coy always washing in ~~NIEPPE~~ ARMENTIERES Allotted washing billets at USINE ELECTRIQUE, NIEPPE Weather stormy & wet. Trenches with 3 feet of water	[illegible] [illegible] See App. VI.
8.1.15 "	No 1 Coy in trenches " 2 " " support 3 " " Reserve 4 " " washing Quiet – trenches very wet weather stormy	
9.1.15 "	Ditto Ditto	
10.1.15	No 3 Coy in trenches, No 4 in support, No 2 Reserve No 1 washing. Weather very wet	Pte KNIGHT H.M. No 9860 killed in action.
11.1.15	Ditto Ditto	

Instructions regarding War Diaries and Intelligence Summaries are contained in F. S. Regs., Part II. and the Staff Manual respectively. Title pages will be prepared in manuscript.

WAR DIARY
or
INTELLIGENCE SUMMARY

(Erase heading not required.)

Army Form C. 2118.

Hour, Date, Place		Summary of Events and Information	Remarks and references to Appendices
12.1.15	PLOEGSTEERT	Enemy shelling severe – weather very wet Warnave River in flood – Wiring & improvement of trenches	Pte 9503 Saunders T. Kd in action
13.1.15	"	2 Coy in trenches, 1 Coy in support, 4 Coy Reserve, 3 Coy Washing Enemy shelling severe.	
14.1.15	"	Ditto – Quiet day – Improvement of trenches	
15.1.15	"	Ditto – Weather improving – " "	
16.1.15	"	4 Coy in trenches, 3 Coy supports 1 Coy Reserve 2 Coy Washing in ARMENTIERES	1 Wounded
17.1.15		Ditto – improvement of trenches & wiring	

1247 W 3299 200,000 (E) 8/14 J.B.C. & A. Forms/C. 2118/11.

Army Form C. 2118.

Instructions regarding War Diaries and Intelligence Summaries are contained in F. S. Regs., Part II. and the Staff Manual respectively. Title pages will be prepared in manuscript.

WAR DIARY
or
INTELLIGENCE SUMMARY
(Erase heading not required.)

Hour, Date, Place	Summary of Events and Information	Remarks and references to Appendices
18.1.15 PLOEGSTEERT	Sniping rather more active – weather very wet – R. WARNAVE v. high	
19.1.15 "	Relief as on 16th inst. " " " " "	
20.1.15 "	Normal situation – weather dryer.	Pte HERBAGE shot in action 1 wounded
21.1.15 "	" " " " & colder	
22.1.15 "	Relief as on 19th 15 men & 2 N.C.Os & 2 Officers 2/Lt HARVEY and ALCOCK arrived as draft.	
23.1.15 "	Finer weather	
24.1.15 "	Sniping active	Pte DANIEL A. K. in action
25.1.15 "	" " weather fine. relief as on 22nd	
26.1.15 "	Instructions received to keep on the look out for any movements of the enemy likely to confirm intention of attack to celebrate Kaisers birthday on 27th	
27.1.15	Quiet day – movement of transport (enemy) reported from S to N. v. cold	Pte GEORGE A.N. wd & died following day. 1 wounded
28.1.15	" " Hard frost. Shelling by our siege battery on houses in front of SOMERSETS and N of LE CHEER relief as on 25th	

1247 W 3299 200,000 (E) 8/14 J.B.C. & A. Forms/C. 2118/11.

Instructions regarding War Diaries and Intelligence Summaries are contained in F. S. Regs., Part II. and the Staff Manual respectively. Title pages will be prepared in manuscript.

WAR DIARY
or
INTELLIGENCE SUMMARY.
(Erase heading not required.)

Army Form C. 2118.

Hour, Date, Place	Summary of Events and Information	Remarks and references to Appendices
29.1.15 PLOEGSTEERT	Drier weather. Quiet day	1/No. 9639 Pte (WEBB, H.?) Capt ...
30.1.15	" " " "	1 wounded x
31.1.15	Reliefs	x Pte No. 9619 ROBBINS S. died from wounds

(73989) W4141—463. 400,000. 9/14. H.&J.Ltd. Forms/C. 2118/10.

Details of Positions of Coys.

DATE	TRENCHES	SUPPORT	RESERVE	NIEPPE
7	1 Coy	2 Coy	3 Coy	4 Coy
8				
9			to wash	to wash
10	3	4	2	1
11			to wash	to wash
12				
13	2	1	4	3
14			to wash	to wash
15				
16	4	3	1	2
17			to wash	to wash
18				
19	1	2	3	4
20			to wash	to wash
21				
22	3	4	2	1
23			to wash	to wash
24				
25	2	1	4	3
26			to wash	to wash
27				
28	4	3	1	2
29			to wash	to wash
30				
31	1	2	3	4

A. C. Oppenheim, Captn.
ADJT. 5th BN. CITY OF LONDON RIFLES.

4th Div.
11th Inf.Bde.

WAR DIARY

5TH BATTN. THE LONDON REGT. (L. R..B.)

F E B R U A R Y

1 9 1 5.

Army Form C. 2118.

Instructions regarding War Diaries and Intelligence Summaries are contained in F. S. Regs., Part II. and the Staff Manual respectively. Title pages will be prepared in manuscript.

WAR DIARY
or
~~INTELLIGENCE SUMMARY.~~

(Erase heading not required.)

Hour, Date, Place		Summary of Events and Information	Remarks and references to Appendices
1.2.15	PLOEGSTEERT	Draft from Base arrived about 4 p.m. Strength 4 Sgts. (2 Corps.) 145 men	[illegible]
		Quiet day. Reported movement of enemy to our front.	
2.2.15		Reported movement of transport to our front. Normal day. Weather fine.	1 wounded
3.2.15		Relief. Very fine day.	9986 Pte WATKINS R.E. Kd
4.2.15		Normal situation	1 wounded
5.2.15		Nothing to report	
6.2.15		Relief	
7.2.15		Nothing to report.	

5th LRB

Instructions regarding War Diaries and Intelligence Summaries are contained in F. S. Regs., Part II. and the Staff Manual respectively. Title pages will be prepared in manuscript.

WAR DIARY
or
INTELLIGENCE SUMMARY
(Erase heading not required.)

Army Form C. 2118.

Hour, Date, Place	Summary of Events and Information	Remarks and references to Appendices
8.2.15 PLOEGSTEERT	Enemy Artillery action.	No 9261 Cpl Schomberg B.H. 1 killed.
9.2.15 "	Relief. Normal situation	
10.2.15 "	Normal	2/Lt R FORBES Killed 1 Wounded
11.2.15 "	Normal	No 9714 Pte Appleton H.W. 1 killed. 2 wounded 4 wounded of whom No 9509 Pte [illegible] died
12.2.15 "	Relief	
13.2.15 "	Normal	
14.2.15 "	Report received through German prisoners that there would be a German attack on night 15th or 16th	5th LRB
15.2.15 "	Relief. Enemy artillery action Took over E LANCS HOUSE	vide appendix XII
16.2.15 "	Normal	No 9312 Pte Gardiner T.P. 1 killed 1 wounded
17.2.15 "	Normal	
18.2.15 "	Relief	2nd Lieut J E ALCOCK wounded
19.2.15 "	Normal	No 973 Pte Stewart A. 1 killed 2 wounded
20.2.15 "	Enemy artillery action. Draft of 1 Corp. 97 men arrived	1 wounded
21.2.15	Relief	1 wounded

1247 W 3299 200,000 (E) 8/14 J.B.C. & A. Forms/C. 2118/11.

Army Form C. 2118.

Instructions regarding War Diaries and Intelligence Summaries are contained in F. S. Regs., Part II. and the Staff Manual respectively. Title pages will be prepared in manuscript.

WAR DIARY
~~or~~
~~INTELLIGENCE SUMMARY~~

(Erase heading not required.)

Hour, Date, Place	Summary of Events and Information	Remarks and references to Appendices
22. February 1915 PLOEGSTEERT	Two officers 2nd Lieuts CHARLES + WHITE joined yesterday from 1st Reserve Battn. Very Misty – An approximate plan of the Trench is attached for future reference. It is self explanatory. Normal situation	Appendix XII
23 " "	New right M.G. Emplacement finished – Left emplacement in course of construction. Several 6" shrapnel fell close to H.Qrs. Method of carrying out work in trench described. 1st case of Cerebro Spinal Meningitis reported. Normal situation	" — 5 men wounded " XIII
24 " "	Relief. Very cold with snow. Four N.C.O.s promoted from the Battn. to commissions in the Battn. viz Co-S-M WALLIS, Co-S-M COTTER, Sgt FLINDT + Cpl RUSSELL – to date 11th inst. Normal situation	
25 " "	Snow on the ground – 2nd case of Cerebro Spinal Meningitis (Suspected) sent away. Confirmed the same evening – Normal situation	5th LRB
26 " "	Very misty morning – German flag in front of Enemy's wire brought in by Cpl JENKINS No 1 Coy. Brigadier General HASLER takes over Command of the Brigade – Normal situation	1 man Wounded
27 " "	Relief – 3rd Case of Cerebro Spinal Meningitis brought in. Died during the morning – a 4th case is reported which was sent away on 23rd inst. 2nd Lt HARVEY takes over Machine Gun Detachment. Our artillery shell PELERIN during the day. A few small shells mostly blind were fired in reply –	2nd Lt FURSDON wounded 1 man wounded No 8810 Cpl HOPKINS died of wounds No 179 Pte POTTER died of cerebro spinal meningitis
28 " "	Very cold + windy – Bright. Left M.G Emplacement completed – Both now waiting for the two extra guns. Normal situation	

[illegible signature], Capt.

1247 W 3299 200,000 (E) 8/14 J.B.C. & A. Forms/C. 2118/11.

APPENDIX XII

L. R. B Trench

not altogether drawn to scale.

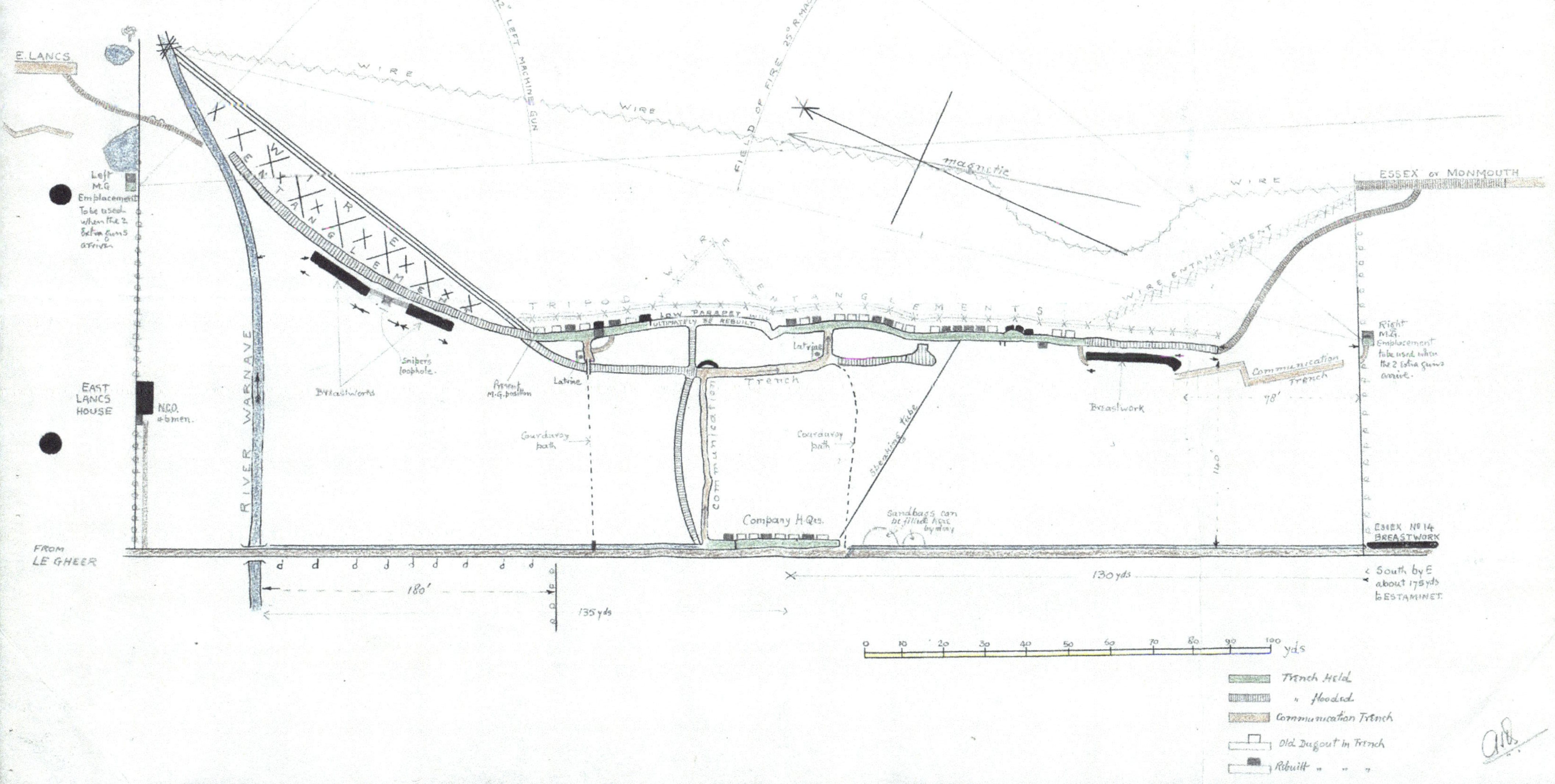

APPENDIX XIII

Method of keeping Trench &c in State of repair

The main points, in order of importance, to which attention has to be paid are

I DEFENCE. Fire positions, Wire &c

II SAFETY OF GARRISON

III COMFORT " "

To ensure continuity in the Work, which would otherwise be difficult as each Company is only in for 3 days, permanent parties are detailed as follows. These assist the O.C Trench, under direction from Head Quarters.

A. Cpl. and 3 men for wiring

B. Cpl and 8 men for revetting, building &c

C Two men for use of pumps & to advise re drainage &c.

The woodwork wanted by B is prepared at Battn H. Qrs & sent up as ready for fixing as possible.

The above system has been found to work very well

[signature]

4th Div.
11th Inf. Bde.

WAR DIARY

5TH BATTN. THE LONDON REGT. (L. R. B.)

M A R C H

1 9 1 5.

Instructions regarding War Diaries and Intelligence Summaries are contained in F. S. Regs., Part II. and the Staff Manual respectively. Title pages will be prepared in manuscript.

WAR DIARY
or
~~INTELLIGENCE SUMMARY~~
(Erase heading not required.)

Army Form C. 2118.

Hour, Date, Place	Summary of Events and Information	Remarks and references to Appendices
PLOEGSTEERT MARCH. 1	The medical officer Major DUCAT RAMC T.F relieved by Lt EDMUNDS RAMC (Temp. Commission) Very stormy afternoon - snow & rain Situation normal	
" 2 "	Relief - very cold - PLOEGSTEERT shelled in afternoon	No 9335 Pte R.L. COOPER Killed 1 man wounded.
" 3 "	Very wet - practically no sniping all day -	
" 4 "	PLOEGSTEERT shelled rather heavily - a six inch incendiary shell came through Headquarters doing considerable damage - The fire caused was put out.	1 man wounded
" 5 "	Relief - very windy - PLOEGSTEERT shelled both morning & afternoon	No 29 Pte C.F. YOUNG Killed " 9742 " GIBSON died in Hospital BOULOGNE " 305 " A.V. BARRETT reported to have died from cerebro spinal meningitis on 28th ult. in No 10. S.H.
" 6 "	Wet - PLOEGSTEERT shelled in the morning -	
" 7 "	Situation normal	

1217 W 3299 200,000 (E) 8/14 J.B.C. & A. Forms/C. 2118/11.

Instructions regarding War Diaries and Intelligence Summaries are contained in F. S. Regs., Part II. and the Staff Manual respectively. Title pages will be prepared in manuscript.

WAR DIARY
or
~~INTELLIGENCE SUMMARY~~
(Erase heading not required.)

Army Form C. 2118.

Hour, Date, Place		Summary of Events and Information	Remarks and references to Appendices
8. 3. 15	PLOEGSTEERT	Relief - very cold - Some snow. Union Jack planted in front of our wire on a mine. arranged by the R.E. Situation normal	1 man wounded.
9. 3. 15	"	very cold - slight shelling - Situation normal	
10. 3. 15	"	very heavy shelling by our Artillery all day - no reply -	
11. 3. 15	"	Relief, heavy shelling by our artillery - no reply -	
12. 3. 15	"	Warm - heavy shelling by our Artillery - no reply - We hand over our Trench to the ESSEX - [1 case of scarlet fever in No 2 Coy]	1115 Pte F B BENNETT wounded & died
13. 3. 15	"	Warm - very quiet day. Situation normal - Visited E. LANCS ~~trf~~ right trench preparatory to taking over on night 16-17. [2nd case of Scarlet fever No 2 Coy -]	1047 Bug. GARTON reported died at ... in 10-3-15 Cerebrospinal meningitis
14. 3. 15	"	Orders rec'd cancelling the new method of holding the Bde Trenches - Further orders rec'd to be prepared to move on night 15-16 - Cancelled owing to attack on 27 Div - Very heavy firing to the North during the Evg: - [Suspicious case (3rd) Scarlet fever No 2 Coy -] mild - WARNAVE LODGE (E-LANCS HOUSE) & RED HOUSE handed over -	APPENDICES XIV. XV. XVI

Instructions regarding War Diaries and Intelligence Summaries are contained in F. S. Regs., Part II. and the Staff Manual respectively. Title pages will be prepared in manuscript.

WAR DIARY
or
~~INTELLIGENCE SUMMARY~~

(Erase heading not required.)

Army Form C. 2118.

Hour, Date, Place	Summary of Events and Information	Remarks and references to Appendices
15.3.15. PLOEGSTEERT	very mild. Situation normal. Ordered to be ready to move tomorrow	
16.3.15 "	Message received 6.50 a.m. by which ordered to be clear of PLOEGSTEERT by 2 pm at 11 am fresh message that orders may be changed to handing over tomorrow night and not to move without further orders – At 1-2 pm "Relief of Brigade will not take place today. Regimental preliminary arrangements may be continued" – at 5-55 pm "All moves cancelled" Mild. C.O. left sick	
17.3.15 "	Situation normal. Took over right trench from E. LANCS Regt 1st Battalion and the support farm	
18.3.15 "	Situation normal	
19.3.15 "	situation normal. cold & snow. Dug new trench in front of convent	
20.3.15 "	Situation normal 1½ inches of snow fell in early morning all melted by 11 am Order received to hand over trench to 1st Battalion ESSEX Regt tonight and to take over 1st Battalion SOMERSET LIGHT INFANTRY trenches and 1st Battalion RIFLE BRIGADE left trench with H.Qrs at RIFLE HOUSE tomorrow – HQrs shelled and hit by 1 shell from field gun.	Copy of Battn Orders of 20.3.15 attached. appendix XVII
21.3.15. PLOEGSTEERT WOOD	Situation normal – fine – took over trenches from S.L.I. & R.B.	
22.3.15 " "	Situation normal – fine –	22.3.15 Killed No 9344 Pte SLATTER F.H. Wounded one
23.3.15 " "	ditto fine morning, wet in afternoon draft of 93 men arrived	23.3.15 Wounded one
24.3.15 " "	ditto wet visited by General Allenby, Admiral Sir Lewis Bayley & staff	

M. [illegible] Capt. LRB

Instructions regarding War Diaries and Intelligence Summaries are contained in F. S. Regs., Part II. and the Staff Manual respectively. Title pages will be prepared in manuscript.

WAR DIARY
or
INTELLIGENCE SUMMARY
(Erase heading not required.)

Army Form C. 2118.

Hour, Date, Place	Summary of Events and Information	Remarks and references to Appendices
25.3.15 PLOEGSTEERT WOOD	Situation normal – Showery – a party of JAPANESE Officers and a RUSSIAN Officer were shown through the wood.	
26.3.15 ditto	Situation normal – fine	
27.3.15 ditto	ditto ditto General Sir HORACE SMITH DORRIEN Comd Second Army visited wood and called at RIFLE HOUSE and expressed to C.O. his regret at not being able to see the Battalion as a whole. He had always heard how well the Battalion had done and wished all ranks to realize how fully their good work was being appreciated. He hoped soon to be able to express his personal thanks to the Battalion. Brigadier & Brigade-Major Commanding Lincoln & Leicester Brigade T.F. came to inspect wood.	27.3.15 Wounded 3
28.3.15 ditto	Situation normal – fine cold – 3 platoons of 4th Battn LINCOLN Regt T.F. attached for instruction in trench work etc under Captain TETLEY. [LORAINE, Foreign Office, from Embassy Paris & Naval Attachee visited wood.]	28.3.15 Wounded 1
29.3.15 ditto	Situation normal fine cold [General BADEN-POWELL visited wood.] 3 further platoons of above Regiment attached for instruction.	29.3.15 Killed No 1109 Pte UNDERHILL F.J.
30.3.15 ditto	Situation normal – fine, cold at night –	
31.3.15 ditto	ditto ditto Sent down Lieut VINCENT & 2nd Lt DOODS to ROUEN to bring up draft)	31.3.15 Killed 3. Capt Morrison, No 309 Pte POWIS W.J., No 191 Pte SHAW A.D. Wounded one

M. Soames Capt LRB

"A" Form. Army Form C. 2121.

MESSAGES AND SIGNALS. No. of Message ______

Prefix SM Code HDAM m.	Words 40	This message is on a/c of:	Recd. at 8.39 p m.
Office of Origin and Service Instructions.	Charge	Service.	Date LRB 14/3/15
11th Inf Bde	Sent At ______ m. To ______ By ______	(Signature of "Franking Officer.")	From ______ By ______

TO { ALL UNITS

Sender's Number	Day of Month	In reply to Number	AAA
BM 172	14th		

The	alteration	in	the	method
of	holding	the	trenches	will
not	now	take	place	AAA
Units	will	be	prepared	to
move	on	night	15-16	after
handing	over	their	trenches	AAA

XIV

From 11th Bde
Place
Time 8.20 a.m.

The above may be forwarded as now corrected. (Z)

Censor. Signature of Addressor or person authorised to telegraph in his name

*This line should be erased if not required.

3662 M. & Co. Ltd. Wt. W929/549—100,000. 6/14. Forms C2121/10.

"A" Form. Army Form C. 2121.

MESSAGES AND SIGNALS. No. of Message

Prefix SM Code 10.40 a.m. Words Charge

Office of Origin and Service Instructions.
11th Inf Brig
Two addresses

This message is on a/c of: Service.

(Signature of "Franking Officer.")

Sent At m. To By

Recd. at 10.5? a m.
Date LRB 14/3/15
From ZK
By a/Cpl Wallis W.7.

TO L R B
E LANCS

Sender's Number	Day of Month	In reply to Number	AAA
B.M.176	14th	LRB 4	

LRB	will	hand	over	WARNAVE
LODGE	to	E.LANCS	to-night	and
RED	HOUSE	during	to-day	AAA
Addressed	LRB	repeated	E	LANCS

XV

From 11th BDE
Place
Time 10.40 AM

The above may be forwarded as now corrected. (Z)

Censor. Signature of Addresser or person authorised to telegraph in his name

*This line should be erased if not required.

8662 M. & Co. Ltd. Wt. W939/549—100,000. 6/14. Forms C2 21/10.

"A" Form.

Army Form C. 2121.

MESSAGES AND SIGNALS.

No. of Message

Prefix S M Code 9.45pm. Words 36 Charge

Office of Origin and Service Instructions: 11th Inf Bde

Sent At m. To By

This message is on a/c of: Service.

(Signature of "Franking Officer.")

Recd. at 9.5x pm.
Date LRB 14/3/15
From ZK
By Rfm. Harris A.

TO ALL UNITS

Sender's Number	Day of Month	In reply to Number	AAA
* B.M. 200	14th.		

Owing	to	the	attack	on
the	27th	Division	now	in
progress	the	relief	of	the
Bde	by	the	83rd	Inf
Bde	is	postponed	till	further
orders				

XVI

From Eleventh Inf Bde
Place
Time 9.45 p.m.

The above may be forwarded as now corrected. (Z)

Censor. Signature of Addressor or person authorised to telegraph in his name

*This line should be erased if not required.

8562 M. & Co. Ltd. Wt. W929/549—100,000. 6/14. Forms C2121/10.

Appendix XVII

Battalion Orders by MAJOR BATES comdg. L.R.B. 20/3/15.

The battn. will hold from the night of the 21st-22nd a line from REGENT STREET (exclusive) to SOMERSET left trench (inclusive) with 3 Coys, each Coy. finding its own supports in TOURIST line + HUNTER AVENUE.
One Company in reserve in billets in PLOEGSTEERT.
The division of this front is as shown on attached sketch, each division being numbered as No1, No2, No3 subsections.
Each subsection will be held by 1 Company.
The numbers shown in red denote the strength of the garrison and will never be less than as shown.
Where the strength of the garrison is not shown in the 2nd and 3rd lines the numbers may be equally divided between the breastworks in TOURIST line and HUNTER AVENUE.

HQRS. will be at RIFLE HOUSE.

ALLOTMENT from night of 21st-22nd will be as follows.

No1 Subsection	1 Coy
No2 "	3 Coy
No3 "	4 Coy
BILLETS	2 Coy

Position of M.G. will be shown to M.G. Officer.

Sequence of Coys. in billets will be 2, 1, 3, 4 Coys.
The Coy in billets will be relieved every 3 days as at present, the Coy coming out of billets taking over the subsection of the Coy. due for billets.
Thus every Coy. will be in its own subsection for 9 days.
O.C. Coys can arrange their own reliefs within their subsections, but the trench in No1 + 2 subsections should be relieved not more than once every 3 days.

DRINKING WATER. will be obtained only from the water carts which will be always at ESSEX FARM.
The water cart horses & drivers will live in ESSEX FARM.

DUMP for rations etc. will be ESSEX FARM.

SICK PARADE will be at 9 a.m. daily outside the Orderly Room. The M.O. will arrange for one of his medical orderly corporals to march the sick men from HQRS. to the dressing station daily.

BUILDING PARTY & W~~ORKING~~IRING PARTY

L/Cpls BELCHER, RICE and STRANSOM will be attached to HQRS.

The remainder of the building & wiring party will return to duty with their coys.

If any building or wiring is required to be done the N.C.O. i/c attached to HQRS as above will ask O.C. Coys for the service of these men.

[signature illegible] Capt.
ADJT. 9TH BN. CITY OF LONDON RIFLES.

4th Div.
11th Inf.Bde.

WAR DIARY

5TH BATTN. THE LONDON REGT. (L. R..B.)

A P R I L

1 9 1 5.

April 1915.

Instructions regarding War Diaries and Intelligence Summaries are contained in F. S. Regs., Part II. and the Staff Manual respectively. Title pages will be prepared in manuscript.

WAR DIARY
or
INTELLIGENCE SUMMARY
(Erase heading not required.)

Army Form C. 2118.

Hour, Date, Place 1915.		Summary of Events and Information	Remarks and references to Appendices
PLOEGSTEERT WOOD	APRIL 1st	Fine - Situation normal. 2 Sgts 4 Cpls + 104 men joined yesterday —	1 Sgt + 4 Men Wounded.
"	2nd	" " " Lord Pembroke brought a party of visitors round -	1 Man Wounded -
"	3rd	Showery " "	
"	4th	" " "	
"	5th	" " " Method of holding our line changed from 3 Coys to 2 Coys + 1 platoon. This allows one Coy to go to ARMENTIERES & leaves 3 platoons in PLOEGSTEERT	
"	6th	Wet " " 8 cadets from the BAILLEUL SCHOOL attached for instruction for 1 night	
"	7th	" " " Further 8 " " " " " " " " " "	
"	8th	Showery " " Genl Sir R. POLE CAREW called - 2 platoons of 5th GLOS. Territorials attached for 1 nights instruction - A case of Cerebro Spinal meningitis (Sgt BEVAN)	251 Pte L. JENKINS Killed. 1 man wounded.
"	9th	Fine " " Capt R.E. OTTER attached to 125 Batt RFA for weeks instruction. 2 more platoons of the 5th GLOS attached for nights instruction -	~~8918 Sgt PEDDELL S.E. Killed~~
"	10th	" " " 2 platoons of the 4th OXF & BUCKS L.I. T.F attached for 1 nights instruction	8918 Sgt PEDDELL S.E. Killed
"	11th	" " " Received news that we were to be relieved on 17/18th. This was "Secret" but the information was public property next day in PLOEGSTEERT	Vide Appendix 18
"	12th	" " "	2nd Lt COTTER Killed
"	13th	" "	
"	14th	Showery "	
"	15th	Fine " Reported by Engineers that they had heard Enemy countermining toward our mine. On investigation the O.C. 170 T.M.C. R.E. threw doubts on the report. C.Os of 7th & 8 WORCESTERS shown round.	
"	16th	Fine " " Two parties of Press Representatives were shown round the wood.	Pte HARRIS Killed
	17th	Relieved by the 7th WORCESTERS T.F.	

1247 W 3299 200,000 (E) 8/14 J.B.C. & A. Forms/C. 2118/11.

April 1915

Instructions regarding War Diaries and Intelligence Summaries are contained in F. S. Regs., Part II. and the Staff Manual respectively. Title pages will be prepared in manuscript.

WAR DIARY
or
INTELLIGENCE SUMMARY
(Erase heading not required.)

Army Form C. 2118.

Hour, Date, Place		Summary of Events and Information	Remarks and references to Appendices
17th (contd)	9:30 pm.	Last Company relieved. Marched to STEENWERCK & went into billets just west of the "Grand Beaumar" on the LE VEAU - STEENWERCK ROAD.	
18th		Fine. Troops rested.	
19th		" Battalion carried out Company Training & Route Marching	
20		" " " "	
21st		" " " "	
22nd		" " " "	
23rd		Fine. Battalion carried out Route March & were inspected while on the march by LT.-GENL PULTENEY commanding III Army Corps. Message received "Prepare to move at short notice" while on march. Subsequent orders to be ready to move @ 3 hours notice & finally at 2 hours notice. Orders for 11th Brigade to entrain received. East Lancs. attached to 12th Brigade.	Vide Appendix 19.

1247 W 3299 200,000 (E) 8/14 J.B.C. & A. Forms/C. 2118/11.

April 1915

Instructions regarding War Diaries and Intelligence Summaries are contained in F. S. Regs., Part II. and the Staff Manual respectively. Title pages will be prepared in manuscript.

WAR DIARY
or
INTELLIGENCE SUMMARY

(Erase heading not required.)

Army Form C. 2118.

Hour, Date, Place		Summary of Events and Information	Remarks and references to Appendices
24th. STEENWERCK.	12.50pm	Orders received to entrain at Station for POPERINGHE. Transport ordered to proceed by road.	Vide appendix. 20
	4.30pm	Arrived POPERINGHE via Hazebrouck. Marched to BUSSEBOOM & prepared to bivouac, Transport having arrived about 7. pm. Informed we were Army Reserve. Later in evening give close billets in farms round.	
25th BUSSEBOOM.	6.A.M.	Marched to VLAMERTINGHE & billeted west end. Under orders of 5th Army Corps & warned to move at short notice.	
	4.30pm	C.O. sent for by Brigadier Hasler & instructed to send two officers to WIELTJE and VERLORENHOCK. to meet Brigadiers on the spot & ascertain situation. Capt Hussey & Lt Johnson detailed.	
	6.15pm	11th Brigade marched - Hants., R.B., Somerset LI, & L.R.B. - skirting north of YPRÉS which was being heavily shelled. Brigade halted in ST JEAN. The two officers reported back to C.O. C.O. sent for by Brigadier & instructed to issue tools & place himself under orders of Col COMPTON. (Somersets).	

Instructions regarding War Diaries and Intelligence Summaries are contained in F. S. Regs., Part II. and the Staff Manual respectively. Title pages will be prepared in manuscript.

WAR DIARY
or
INTELLIGENCE SUMMARY
(Erase heading not required.)

Army Form C. 2118.

Hour, Date, Place		Summary of Events and Information	Remarks and references to Appendices
25th ST JEAN. (contd)	9.pm.	Tools issued. 3 horses killed by shell. Marched in rear of Somersets L.I. thro' WIELTJE and FORTUIN to about Point - D 13 c 3.8 - under shell fire	
26th	2.A.M.	Commenced digging in, trench facing N.E.	
	3.30 AM	Trench completed at daylight. No definite information whether Battn was in front or 2nd line.	
		Fine. Heavy shelling all day, enfilade & direct fire.	For casualties see summarised list for Month attached. Appendix No. 21.
	noon.	Ordered by Brigade to send Company - as strong as possible - to join up between Hants left & Somerset right. Major Burnell reconnoitred & reported he could not find left of Hants, ground was being heavily shelled, & it would entail very serious loss to attempt this in daylight.	
	4.10pm	Brigade sanctioned movement being delayed till nightfall. Later in afternoon Battn ordered to move at dusk & join up the R.B. right & Hants left neither point being indicated. Battn marched to Wood D 20 a c. where it was known the R.B. were entrenched. Met Gunner Officer who	

1247 W 3299 200,000 (E) 8/14 J.B.C. & A. Forms/C. 2118/11.

April 1915

Instructions regarding War Diaries and Intelligence Summaries are contained in F. S. Regs., Part II. and the Staff Manual respectively. Title pages will be prepared in manuscript.

WAR DIARY
or
INTELLIGENCE SUMMARY
(Erase heading not required.)

Army Form C. 2118.

Hour, Date, Place	Summary of Events and Information	Remarks and references to Appendices
26th (contd).	said Hants line ran EAST & WEST thro' north of D 15.ab. near GRAVENSTAFEL. He reported the Germans had got thro' the gap, but that small mixed party (about 300 under ....) were holding on in the centre. Battn then marched to Point on road D 20 b 8.0 – & C.O. & Capt HUSEY proceeded on to try & ascertain position & met Col BRIDGEFORD (Shropshire L.I.) who was in command of 2½ Battalions (names unknown) & O.C. Mixed Party. Col BRIDGEFORD said he would join up right of Mixed Party & left of Hants & instructed L.R.B. to join up right of R.B. with left of Mixed Party. As line of R.B. was not suitable L.R.B. joined up left flank of R.B. & Mixed Party & dug in on line – Point D 14 d 7.2 to Point D 20 b.2 – north of the Road & facing NORTH. Heavy shelling all night. Several Casualties.	For casualties see summarised list for Month attached. Appendix No 21.
27th	Fine. Heavy shelling all day. Brigadier Genl HASLER killed. Our casualties large. Regmtl S.M. killed & 2 officers wounded.	

1247 W 3299 200,000 (E) 8/14 J.B.C. & A. Forms/C. 2118/11.

April 1915.

Instructions regarding War Diaries and Intelligence Summaries are contained in F. S. Regs., Part II. and the Staff Manual respectively. Title pages will be prepared in manuscript.

WAR DIARY
or
INTELLIGENCE SUMMARY
(Erase heading not required.)

Army Form C. 2118.

Hour, Date, Place	Summary of Events and Information	Remarks and references to Appendices
28th	Line. Shelling continued heavy & very accurate from four quarters N, NE, NW, & S.E. No. 3 Company took over the trench from Mixed Party on the right. R.B. dug across our front & joined up between the Somersets & Hants in the front line. L.R.B. then became 2nd line.	
29th	Line. Shelling not so heavy, but Battn. No. 2 trench badly shelled & also left half of line. Received orders about 7.30 pm. to take over trenches N. of road - D13 c.3 to D13 centre - & relieve 4th EAST YORKS. Two Companies 4th YORK'S attached to Battn. Relief effected. order of Coys. from left. - No. 7 Co., No. 2 Co., No. 3 Co., No. 4 Co., L.R.B. & Z Co. 4th Yorks - with ~~X~~ Y Co. 4th Yorks in support trench dug by Battn. on night of 25th. Battn. left of Brigade line, joined up with ROYAL IRISH - right of 10th Brigade. Capt Otter & 2nd Lt Beard wounded.	For Casualties see summarised list for month attached Appendix No. 21.
30th	Line. Shelling not so heavy. Situation normal. Improved trenches and in places dug new ones as those taken over were very bad.	

1247 W 3299 200,000 (E) 8/14 J.B.C. & A. Forms/C. 2118/11.

"C" Form (Original). Army Form C. 2123.

MESSAGES AND SIGNALS. No. of Message

Prefix Code Words	Received	Sent, or sent out	Office Stamp.
£ s. d. Charges to collect	From By	At m. To	XVIII
Service Instructions. SECRET Secretly hand		By	

Handed in at Office COPY m. Received m.

TO: SOM. L.I. – E. LANCS – HANTS – RIF. BRIG. – LON. RIF. BRIG.

*Sender's Number	Day of Month	In reply to Number	AAA
	11-4-15		

1. The 1st S. MIDLAND BRIGADE from the area STEENWERCK (Excl) NOOTE BOOM will relieve the 11th Inf. Bde less L.R.B on the night 15-16 April. Preliminary arrangements for this relief will be carried out on the night 14/15. The 11th Inf. Bde less L.R.B on relief will move to area STEENWERCK (Excl.) NOOTE BOOM. Details of movement will be issued later.
2. On the night 17/18 the L.R.B will be relieved by a Unit of the S. MIDLAND DIVISION & will then rejoin the 11th Inf. Bde.
3. Detail of stores etc that are to be handed over with the trenches to the relieving units attached

Signed typewritten G H Martin
Bry. Maj. 11. I. B
Capt.

Issued at 7 PM.

FROM

PLACE & TIME

* This line should be erased if not required.

W.3384—583. 80,000 Pads—8/14. S. B. Ltd.—Forms/C.2123.

"C" Form (Original). Army Form C. 2123.

MESSAGES AND SIGNALS. No. of Message.........

Prefix......... Code......... Words.........

£ s. d.

Charges to collect

Service Instructions.

Received From......... By.........

Sent, or sent out At.........m. To......... By.........

Office Stamp.

19

Handed in at Copy Office.........m. Received.........m.

TO All Units 11th Inf. Bde

*Sender's Number	Day of Month	In reply to Number	AAA
	23 April		

1. The 11th Infantry Brigade will be prepared to move to POPERINGHE by rail.
2. Som: L. I & HANTS less transport & horses will entrain at BAILLEUL. RIFLE BRIGADE. & L.R.B. under Major SEYMOUR RIF. BRIG. will entrain at STEENWERCK.
2. The M. G. Sections complete with S.A.A. Carts together with 5 SAA Carts per battn will entrain at BAILLEUL under Lt BENNETT Som. L. I. in a train specially composed. The remaining transport & horses of the Bde will proceed to POPERINGHE by march route. 3 hours notice will be given before departure of first train wh. start from BAILLEUL. The interval between departure of trains will be half an hour.
3. The Transport of the Bde, less M. G. & SAA carts under Lt BARCLAY R. B will be held in readiness to march at half an hour's notice after 3 PM.
4. Supply wagons will march full.

Please acknowledge.

FROM 11th Inf. Brig.

PLACE & TIME

* This line should be erased if not required.

W.3384—583. 80,000 Pads—8/14. S. B. Ltd.—Forms/C.2123.

(20)

Copy No 5

OPERATION ORDER No 1
by
Brig. Genl J. HASLER Comdg 11 Inf Bde — 24 April

1. The Brigade will move tomorrow to VLAMERTINGHE, by the direct road G.7.C and on arrival will go into billets.

2. Order of march SOM L I – HANTS – RIF BRIG – L R B
Starting point road junction G 7 c North

3. The Brigade will march at 6 am. The first echelon transport will move with Battns. The Second echelons will move brigaded under Lt BARCLAY. R.B. in rear of the L.R.B.
Bearer Subdivision 12th Field Ambulance will move in rear of the Column.

4. Brigade after reaching VLAMERTINGHE will be ready to move at short notice

5. Supply wagons will refill at BUSSEBOOM, and will move to VLAMERTINGHE as soon as they have done so

W.H.M. FREESTON Capt
for
Brig Maj. 11th Inf Bde

9.35 pm

Issued to Som. L I – HANTS
R.B – L.R.B – 12th Fd Amb

Casualties for April 1915

Appendix 21

CASUALTIES. APRIL 1915

Date	Killed in Action	Killed (Continued)	Names (Officers) + number other ranks Wounded
APRIL 1	—	-	5 men wounded
" 2	—	-	1 man "
" 8	251 Pte. JENKINS. L.	-	1 " "
" 10	8918 Sgt. PEDDELL SE	-	-
" 12	2nd LT G. H. COTTER	-	-
" 15	616 Pte. HARRIES T. J.	-	-
" 16	—	-	1 " " (slight)
" 26.	7 107 Pte THACKRAH C.G. 396 " CROMPTON W.G. 793 " PEPPER J.W. 222 " TUCKER R.C. 874 " WOODWARD H.E. 237 " STOREK R. 971 " HOTTEN H.J.	-	22 men "
" 27	19 8913 Pte CHARLES W.G. 9455 " PERCY W.R.M. 605 " BROWN L.V. 116 " FISK E. 9796 " COOPER H.C. 9389 L/Sgt FURRELL L. 1564 Pte MORRIS E 793 " ROBINSON R. 640 " FALLAIZE A.T. 9897 " LANDSBERG G. 954 " PEARSON C. R. B. 1059 " HAWKINS W. S. B. 220 L/Cpl. VASEY G.E. 1155 Pte DIXON W.H. 8616 Coy. S.M. THOMAS G.D. 1098 Pte. JUZI G.E.T. F.	287 Pte. WHITE J.E. 9985 " LOOSELEY W. 986 " HEAVINGHAM H.H. —	2 LIEUT. B.S. HARVEY (w) " L.E. WHITEHEAD " + 76 men wounded
28.	6 9793 Reg. S. Major. HARRINGTON A.G. 9594 L/Cpl. READING J.W.C. 9563 Pte. PIGDEN A.R.	492 Pte. FOSTER A.J. 282 " NEWELL J.G. 863 " HEWITT J.E. (9512 Pte. C.M. BELL died of wounds)	1 LIEUT E.T. EDMUNDS (RAMC) M.O. +10 men wounded.
29.	— Notice Received 324 L/Cpl. WRIGHT, N.C.B. - died of wounds 904 Pte ESCARE C.A. "	—	CAPT. R.E. OTTER, 2 LT. BEARD H.C. 2 + ~~12~~ 15 men wounded
30.	— Notice Received Pte RIMINGTON E.W. died of wounds	—	1 wounded

4th Div.
11th Inf.Bde.

WAR DIARY

5th BATTN. THE LONDON REGT. (L.R.B.)

M A Y

1 9 1 5.

(to G. H. Q. 28..5..15.)

May 1915.

Instructions regarding War Diaries and Intelligence Summaries are contained in F. S. Regs., Part II. and the Staff Manual respectively. Title pages will be prepared in manuscript.

WAR DIARY
or
~~INTELLIGENCE~~ SUMMARY
(Erase heading not required.)

Army Form C. 2118.

Hour, Date, Place		Summary of Events and Information	Remarks and references to Appendices
1st Trenches.		In trenches N. of road in D 13.c. Shelling continued. Confidential Orders received stating how to act in case of withdrawal. No alteration.	
2nd Do		Heavy shelling all day. Small cottage 100 yds in front of left Co set on fire.	
	5.20 pm	Heavy shelling on left & our front. Gas seen issuing from German trenches. Capt HUSEY took over command of Support trench.	
	5.40.	Bombardment still on. Gas blown off. Casualties very heavy in No 7. Co. Two platoons Y. Co. 4th Yorks were sent up between No 4. & Z Co. 4th Yorks.	For casualties see summarised list for month attached Appendix No. 35.
	9. pm	Capt SMITH & 70 men EAST LANCS brought up 35 boxes S.A.A. & took over support trench, remaining platoons of Y. Co reinforced front line.	
	M'night	Two prisoners were captured - one 33rd & one 234th Regmts, 102 Brigade. 51. Res. Division 26th Corps. Casualties very heavy. - 45 killed, 8 officers & 120 men wounded -	
3rd Do	2.45 AM.	Remainder of Co. EAST LANCS came up to support & two platoons relieved No 11. & 14. Platoons in front line.	
	3.30. AM	Found Germans had dug in all along our front about 200 yards away under cover of gas & shelling.	

1247 W 3299 200,000 (E) 8/14 J.B.C. & A. Forms/C. 2118/11.

May 1915.

Instructions regarding War Diaries and Intelligence Summaries are contained in F. S. Regs., Part II. and the Staff Manual respectively. Title pages will be prepared in manuscript.

WAR DIARY
or
INTELLIGENCE SUMMARY
(Erase heading not required.)

Army Form C. 2118.

Hour, Date, Place		Summary of Events and Information	Remarks and references to Appendices
3rd (contd)	9. A.M.	Two Machine Guns out of action. Intermittent shelling all day. Received orders for withdrawal of Brigade & attached troops. L.R.B. being last to move @ 12.45 A.M. on the morning of the 4th. Lieut Price & 2nd Lt. R. Lintott killed.	Casualties April 25 - May 4 Officers / NCOs & men KILLED 2 / 77 WOUNDED 12. / 246 MISSING - / 9 SICK 2. / 60 16 . 392.
4th	12.45 AM.	Withdrawal commenced & carried out without any casualties. Marched to ELVERDINGHE - B 14.c. - via Pontoon Bridge No 2 - & arrived @ 5 A.M.	
ELVERDINGHE.	5.0. A.M.		
"	7.30 pm.	Brigade moved [L.R.B. leading] to bivouac in Wood A.30 centre. [Brigade congratulated by Brigadier.	Brigade Order vide Appendix No 22.
5th 2 Wood.		Bivouac in Wood. [Fine rather cold. LT. MOYES (R.A.M.C) joined.	
6th	Do	" " " "	
7th	Do	" " " " General Sir Herbert Plumer commanding 5th Army Corps in company with Major General Wilson IV Division visited the Regiment.	
8th	Do.	Batt'n promised 4 days rest & marched to Wood A 16 a. & bivouaced. Captain Charles of 4th Div'n Staff brought	

1247 W 3299 200,000 (E) 8/14 J.B.C. & A. Forms/C. 2118/11.

~~April 1915~~ May 1915.

Instructions regarding War Diaries and Intelligence Summaries are contained in F. S. Regs., Part II. and the Staff Manual respectively. Title pages will be prepared in manuscript.

WAR DIARY
or
INTELLIGENCE SUMMARY
(Erase heading not required.)

Army Form C. 2118.

Hour, Date, Place		Summary of Events and Information	Remarks and references to Appendices
May 8th	11.0. pm	orders for Battn to be at IV Divl. H.Q. @ Chateau VLAMERTINGHE by 6 A.M. tomorrow.	
9th	5.45 A.M.	Battn arrived VLAMERTINGHE.	
	8.30 pm.	Fatigue party 300 men (whole battalion) proceeded to dig trenches in C.26.	
10.	8.30. pm.	Ditto Ditto. During the day Battn in Chateau grounds.	
11.		Battn occupied position on bank of stream west of Canal (in the evening) - H.1.b - Ground in most filthy condition - old French lines -	
12.		Ordered to relieve Dublin Fusiliers in front line & take over certain defended posts.. [Brigade Orders vide	Appendix. No. 23.
	8.30 pm	Battalion moved accordingly. [Battalion Orders vide	Do No. 24.
13.	4.0 a.m.	Heavy shelling started & continued incessantly for over 12 hours.	
	5.0 a.m.	18th Hussars on right commenced retiring from their trench. These were prevailed upon to return.	
	6.43 A.M.	Brigade instructed "WIELTJE & the line to be held at all cost" 2 Cos. Kings Own at LA BRIQUE in support.	

Instructions regarding War Diaries and Intelligence Summaries are contained in F. S. Regs., Part II. and the Staff Manual respectively. Title pages will be prepared in manuscript.

WAR DIARY
or
INTELLIGENCE SUMMARY

(Erase heading not required.)

Army Form C. 2118.

Hour, Date, Place		Summary of Events and Information	Remarks and references to Appendices
13th (contd).	7.20 am	Ordered by Brigadier to send up Reserve Co. to act in close support.	vide Brigade Order. Appendix No. 25.
	7.44 ..	20 men of No. 4. sent up to trench & having sent up further reinforcements, reported to Brigade only 20 men left in reserve & asked for 2. Cos. Kings Own to be sent up.	
	8.20 ..	30 men returned from trench reporting no room, so only one Co. Kings Own came up.	
	8.44 ..	Remainder of No. 2. & 4. Cos. sent up & laid behind trenches in close support.	
	8.46 ..	Message received from Capt SOMERS-SMITH. (O.C. trench) that he could hold on easily.	
	9 45. .	Battn. no supports. Brigade sent the other Co. Kings Own. to support Essex.	
	noon	Enemy massed & were heavily fired on by our rifles & machine guns. Enemy's infantry did not make attack.	
	6 30 pm.	Orders for Relief - vide Brigade Orders. B.M. 115 attached.	Appendix No. 26.
	night	Moved to Divisional Support Line immediately across ST JEAN - WIELTJE ROAD opposite our Reserve trench. Casualties very severe. - 2 Officers & 33 men killed; 4 officers & 49 men wounded.	For Casualties see summarised list attached Appendix No. 35.

1247 W 3299 200,000 (E) 8/14 J.B.C. & A. Forms/C. 2118/11.

May 1915.

Instructions regarding War Diaries and Intelligence Summaries are contained in F. S. Regs., Part II. and the Staff Manual respectively. Title pages will be prepared in manuscript.

WAR DIARY
or
INTELLIGENCE SUMMARY
(Erase heading not required.)

Army Form C. 2118.

Hour, Date, Place	Summary of Events and Information	Remarks and references to Appendices
May 14.	Quite day, but 1 killed & 3 men wounded by shell.	
4 pm.	Div^l line to be re-adjusted. vide B.M. No. 153. attached	Appendix No. 27
10. pm.	Moved to 4th Div^l. 2nd support line across Road. N. of IRISH FARM in C.27.a. in accordance with orders.	
May 15.	Quite day 3 men hit by shell.	
11.40 AM	Two Cos. NORTHUMBERLAND FUSILIERS attached. in charge of Major HEADLEY & Capt. & Adjt. BARRETT. - B.M. 220 attached	Appendix No. 28.
12.30 pm.	Received B.M. 621. (attached) with orders for Relief.	vide Appendix No. 29.
night.	Batt^n moved to IV Div^s 1st support line in accordance with orders. Line running roughly from farm in centre of C20 thro' centre of C.21.	
May 16.	Quiet day. Received Orders for move to East bank of CANAL North of No. 2 Pontoon. vide B.M 664. attached Moved at night accordingly.	Appendix No. 30.
May 17	Quiet day. Digging fatigue on 11th Brigade H.Q. dug outs.	
18,	" " D^o D^o	

Instructions regarding War Diaries and Intelligence Summaries are contained in F. S. Regs., Part II. and the Staff Manual respectively. Title pages will be prepared in manuscript.

WAR DIARY
or
INTELLIGENCE SUMMARY
(Erase heading not required.)

Army Form C. 2118.

Hour, Date, Place	Summary of Events and Information	Remarks and references to Appendices
May 19. 4.55 pm.	Quiet day. Orders received that Batt^n to be withdrawn from IV Division owing to severe casualties & sent to TATINGHEM, near St. Omer.	
5.50 pm.	Brigade Orders B.M. 52 received with orders to march to VLAMERTINGHE. vide	B.M. 50 attached. Appendix No 31. Appendix No. 32.
7.30 pm.	Moved to VLAMERTINGHE & spent night in Billets. The 2 Cos. Northumberland Fusiliers attached to East Lancs. Received "Farewell order" from Brigadier-General PROWSE.	vide. Appendix No. 33.
May 20. VLAMERTINGHE.	Inspected & addressed by Major-General WILSON. @ 9.30 AM Batt^n moved off in Motor Bus (20) & arrived at TATTINGHEM. & billeted in the village. Total Strength of Batt^n reduced to:- Officiers 19, Other Ranks 343, 362.	
May 21. TATINGHEM.	Fine. Troops resting in Billets.	
" 22 "	Fine. " " " " Cos. Refitted & new clothing issued.	

1247 W 3299 200,000 (E) 8/14 J.B.C. & A. Forms/C. 2118/11.

Instructions regarding War Diaries and Intelligence Summaries are contained in F. S. Regs., Part II. and the Staff Manual respectively. Title pages will be prepared in manuscript.

WAR DIARY
or
~~INTELLIGENCE SUMMARY~~

(Erase heading not required.)

Army Form C. 2118.

Hour, Date, Place	Summary of Events and Information	Remarks and references to Appendices
May 23. TATINGHEM	Fine. Battn attended Church Parade. Captain Lintott rejoined from England.	
" 24. "	Fine. Coys refitted & Company Training.	
" 25. "	Fine. Company Training. 16. N.C.O. & men rejoin from Base Camp ROUEN.	
" 26. "	Fine. Company Training.	
" 27. "	" " "	
" 28. "	" " " Received Orders for organisation of Composite Battalion - L.R.B, Rangers (1/12) & Kensingtons (1/13) to take duty on Lines of Communication relieving 6th Welsh. L.R.B. to find Southern Railheads.	vide Appendix No. 34..
"	Orders received from G.H.Q. that No 6968 Signaller-Sergt E.A. ADAMS. had been awarded the D.C.M. "for acts of gallantry and devotion in the field".	G.H.Q. orders. dated 22nd May.
" 29. "	Fine. Troops resting. 3. Machine Guns returned to A.O.D.	
" 30 "	Fine. Church Parade in conjunction with Ranger (1/12 London) & Kensingtons (1/13. London).	
" 31 " 7 AM.	Fine. Troops moved to relieve 6th Welsh at Southern Railheads. as shown in Appendix No 34. Entrained at ST. OMER 8 45 AM. H.Q. TRANPORT & Details. remain at TATINGHEM.	

1247 W 3299 200,000 (E) 8/14 J.B.C. & A. Forms/C. 2118/11.

"C" Form (Duplicate). Army Form C. 2123.

MESSAGES AND SIGNALS. No. of Message

Charges to Pay. £ s. d. | Office Stamp. 22

Service Instructions.

Handed in at COPY. Office m. Received m.

TO ALL UNITS

Sender's Number	Day of Month	In reply to Number	AAA
BM 2	4 May.		

Brigade order :- By BRIG - GEN. C. B. PROWSE CMDG. 11th INF. BRIG.

The Brigadier wishes to congratulate the 11th Infantry Brigade on the gallant way they have held their position during the past few days under most trying circumstances.

He also congratulates them on the skillful way in which the most difficult and dangerous operation of a withdrawal at night was carried out.

He wishes above to be communicated to all ranks. He will be glad to receive the names of any Officers - NCO or men that COs wish to bring forward for special mention

FROM Eleventh Inf Bde

PLACE & TIME

W.3394—583. 80,000 Pads—8/14. S. B. Ltd.—Forms/C.2123.

"C" Form (Original). Army Form C. 2123.

MESSAGES AND SIGNALS.

No. of Message

Prefix Code Words	Received	Sent, or sent out	Office Stamp.
£ s. d. Charges to collect	From / By	At m. / To / By	23
Service Instructions.			

Handed in at COPY Office m. Received m.

TO LRB - E LANCS - ESSEX - 1st CAV DIV.

*Sender's Number	Day of Month	In reply to Number	AAA
76	12th May		

The 11th Bde will take over the bit of line now held by DUBLINS in square C 23c AAA The 1st CAV DIV will take over the FORTUIN - WIELTJE Road and 100 yds North of it AAA LRB will hold this front with 2 Coys 150 men AAA The LRB will also take over ~~the~~ and occupy the 4 defended posts round WIELTJE VILLAGE AAA a machine gun & about 20 men in each post AAA Remainder of LRB and HQ will be from right of the ESSEX FM C 28a exclusive to ST JEAN - WIELTJE road inclusive AAA addressed LRB repeated E LANCS - ESSEX and 1st CAV DIV.

FROM 11th Inf Bde

PLACE & TIME 10.30 am

* This line should be erased if not required.

W.2834—585. 30,000 Pads—8/14. S. B. Ltd.—Forms/C.2123.

"A" Form. Army Form C. 2121.

MESSAGES AND SIGNALS. No. of Message

Prefix ...... Code ...... m. Office of Origin and Service Instructions.	Words	Charge	This message is on a/c of: ...... Service. (Signature of "Franking Officer.")	Recd. at ...... m. Date ...... From ...... By ......
	Sent At ...... m. To ...... By		24	

TO Batt^n Orders by MAJOR BATES Comdg L.R.B

Sender's Number.	Day of Month	In reply to Number	
*	12-5-15		AAA

1. The L.R.B will take over (a) the bit of line now held by DUBLINS in Square C 23 c with a minimum of 150 men. (b) also take over and occupy the 3 defended posts round WIELTJE VILLAGE with a garrison of about 20 men in each post (c) remainder of L.R.B and HQ will be from right of ESSEX FARM C 28 a Exclusive to ST JEAN - WIELTJE Road inclusive.
2. No 1 + 2 Coys will take over (a) No 3 Coy (b) No 4 (c)
3 The Batt^n will be ready to move off at 8.30 pm in the following order 1.2.3.4. M Guns ---- Guides will be provided by DUBLINS + S.LANCS + Capt HUSEY will supervise the taking over of the front line.
4. M.G Officer will arrange to have 1 MG in front trench and 1 in 2 of the 3 defended posts round WIELTJE He will use his discretion as to putting his 4th MG either in front trench or in a position commanding exit out of WIELTJE at S end of HQ + No 4 Coy Trench.

From

Place

Time

The above may be forwarded as now corrected. Censor. (Z) Signature of Addressor or person authorised to telegraph in his name.

* This line should be erased if not required.

(632) —McC. & Co. Ltd., London.— W 11400/2045. 100,000 2/15. Forms C 2121/10.

"A" Form. Army Form C. 2121.

MESSAGES AND SIGNALS. No. of Message

Prefix ... Code ... m. / Office of Origin and Service Instructions.	Words	Charge	This message is on a/c of: ... Service.	Recd. at ... m.
	Sent			Date 24
	At ... m.			From
	To			
	By		(Signature of "Franking Officer.")	By

TO Balt[illegible] 12/5/15 page 2.

Sender's Number. *	Day of Month	In reply to Number	AAA

5. The Transport Officer will arrange to have his dump on WIELTJE - ST JEAN road at end of HQ trench C 28 a 8. He should arrange to bring rations on pack animals via bridge 2. LABRIQUE - junction of roads C 27 c 8.7 whence there is a path direct to ESSEX FM middle of C 28 a.

6. Coys will arrange to draw rations from the dump after midnight also water from the water cart.

7. The T.O. will arrange to have a filled water cart at the dump.

8. Coys will carry the tools now in their possession.

Signed A. Coppenheim
Capt & Adj

1 Copy sent to T.O. + QM.

From

Place

Time

The above may be forwarded as now corrected. (Z)

Censor. Signature of Addressor or person authorised to telegraph in his name.

* This line should be erased if not required.

(632) —McC. & Co. Ltd., London.— W 11460-2045. 100,000. 2/15. Forms C 2121/10.

"C" Form (Original). Army Form C. 2123.

MESSAGES AND SIGNALS. No. of Message

Prefix ...... Code ...... Words ...... £ s. d.

Charges to collect

Service Instructions. ZK Priority

Received From ...... By ......

Sent, or sent out At ......m. To ...... By ......

Office Stamp. 25

Handed in at ...... Office 7.20 m. Received 7.45 a m.

TO L R B

*Sender's Number	Day of Month	In reply to Number	AAA
BM 64	13th May		

Send your reserve Company up to act in close support of your front line moving under cover and report situation

FROM 11th Inf. Bry.

PLACE & TIME 7 20 AM

* This line should be erased if not required.

W.2384—583. 80,000 Pads—8/14. S. B. Ltd.—Forms/C.2123.

"C" Form (Original). Army Form C. 2123.

MESSAGES AND SIGNALS. No. of Message

Prefix ... Code ... Words ...	Received	Sent, or sent out	Office Stamp.
£ s. d.	From	At ... m.	26
Charges to collect	By	To	
Service Instructions.		By	

Handed in at COPY Office ... m. Received ... m.

TO ROYAL IRISH – ESSEX – LRB – HANTS – KINGSOWN – RIF BRIG – MONS – SOUTH LANCS –

*Sender's Number	Day of Month	In reply to Number	AAA
BM 115	13 May		

Royal IRISH will take over line now held by RIF BRIG with the right on SHELL TRACK FM RIF.BRIG. moving to CANAL BANK AAA KINGSOWN will take over from L.R.B including defended posts at WIELTJE AAA LRB move to right of Divisional Support line AAA ESSEX will on relief by CAVALRY and Units with whom they are now mixed occupy the Divisional Support line held by them this morning SOUTH LANCS will reorganise and occupy the entrenchment in rear of SHELL TRAP FARM applying to EAST LANCS for guides AAA The Company at present with RIF BRIG can only be moved with consent of ROY IRISH AAA MONMOUTHS find carrying parties 50 men each for HANTS and EAST LANCS these parties will report to STAFF CAPT at LA BRIQUE at nine pm remaining Units stand fast AAA Acknowledge AAA

FROM 11th Inf Brig

PLACE & TIME 6 25 pm

* This line should be erased if not required.

W.3284—583. 30,000 Pads—8/14. S. B. Ltd.—Forms/C.2123.

"C" Form (Original). Army Form C. 2123.

MESSAGES AND SIGNALS. No. of Message

Prefix ... Code ... Words ... £ s. d. Charges to collect	Received From ... By ...	Sent, or sent out At ... m. To ... By ...	Office Stamp.
Service Instructions.			(27)

Handed in at COPY Office ... m. Received ... m.

TO: Som. L.I. - HANTS - E. LANCS - RB - LRB - ESSEX - KINGS OWN MONMOUTHS - S. LANCS - 6 N. FUS - ROY IR - and 12 Bde LANCS FUS - and 7 N. FUS. through 12 Bde

*Sender's Number	Day of Month	In reply to Number	AAA
BM 153	14th May		

In order to readjust the 4th Div. line the following moves will take place tonight AAA MONS will temporarily absorb 2 Coys of 7 North FUS. and will move from LA BRIQUE at 9 PM to take over from E LANCS SHELLTRAP FM inclusive to 100 yds North of road C 22 b. South East AAA KINGS OWN will temporarily absorb 2 Coys 7 North Fus. and will hold the line from the right of the MONMOUTHS to halfway between WIELTJE - ST JULIEN and WIELTJE - FORTUIN Road where they will connect with the 10th Bde AAA The KINGS OWN are to hold the defence posts about WIELTJE VILLAGE AAA The S LANCS will remain in the retrenchment and will withdraw the Coy. now with Roy. IRISH Regt leaving 2 M.GS at disposal of Roy IRISH Regt AAA The E LANCS will on relief by MONS move into the Divnl. Support line WEST of road junction C 21 d. 7.6 AAA The LANCS FUS will move to LA BRIQUE under arrangements made by 12th Bde AAA HANTS will temporarily absorb 2 Coys and M.G. Section 6 NORTH FUS these Coys will move at 9 PM with guides found by Brig: H.Q. AAA The L.R.B will move into Div 2nd line across the road in C 27 a moving at 10 PM by Companies AAA Stand fast Som. L.I. - ESSEX - & Roy. IRISH Regt AAA up till 12 midnight 14/15 reports to 11th Inf Bde HQ AAA Acknowledge

FROM: 11th Inf Bde

PLACE & TIME: 20 PM

* This line should be erased if not required.

W. 2334—583. 30,000 Pads—8/14. S. B. Ltd.—Forms/C. 2123.

"C" Form (Original). Army Form C. 2123.

MESSAGES AND SIGNALS. No. of Message

Prefix Code Words	Received	Sent, or sent out	Office Stamp.
£ s. d.	From	At m.	28
Charges to collect	By	To	
Service Instructions.		By	

Handed in at COPY Office m. Received m.

TO 6 NORTHUMBERLAND FUSILIERS
L R B

*Sender's Number	Day of Month	In reply to Number	AAA
BM 220	15th May		

The 2 Companies of the NORTH FUS now on CANAL BANK will be attached to the L.R.B AAA The L.R.B will send an officer to get in touch with the 6 NORTH FUS whose HQrs are now with the R.B on CANAL BANK and arrange for the Companies to join the L R B after dusk tonight

Repeated 6th NORTH and L R B

FROM 11th Inf Brig
PLACE & TIME 11 40 am

* This line should be erased if not required.

W.3864—583. 30,000 Pads—8/14. S. B. Ltd.—Forms/C.2123.

"C" Form (Original). Army Form C. 2123.

MESSAGES AND SIGNALS. No. of Message..........

Prefix........ Code........ Words........	Received	Sent, or sent out	Office Stamp.
£ s. d. Charges to collect	From........	At........m.	29
Service Instructions.	By........	To........	
		By........	

Handed in at........ COPY ....Office........m. Received........m.

TO KINGS OWN, R IRISH, LAN FUS. ESSEX. MONMOUTHS. S LANCS. Som L.I. RB HANTS. LRB E LANCS

*Sender's Number	Day of Month	In reply to Number	AAA
BM 621	15 May		

Following reliefs take place tonight AAA a Battn 10th Brigade relieves KINGS OWN AAA a Battn 10 Brigade relieves S LANCS AAA LANCS FUS relieve R IRISH west of SHELL TRAP FARM AAA LRB reinforced by two Companies 6th Bn North: Fus relieve E LANCS in 4th Divnl. Support Line AAA On relief KINGS OWN will return to B27 AAA The SOUTH LANCS to west End of 4th Divnl Second line AAA R IRISH to LA BRIQUE AAA E. LANCS to CANAL BANK South of No 2 Bridge AAA Guides to be sent as follows – KINGS OWN to report to Brig: H Q most convenient spot for 9 PM AAA S. LANCS & Royal IRISH Regt old H Q FARM on road in C 27 a. AAA LRB to arrange direct with E LANCS AAA LRB will leave guides at Cross Roads C 21 C to show S. LANCS the trenches 4th Divnl Support line which they vacate AAA Following Units no move Som L I HANTS, RB. MONMOUTHS ESSEX AAA Acknowledge AAA Addressed all Battns in 11th & 12th Brigades

FROM 12th Brigade

PLACE & TIME 12.30 pm

* This line should be erased if not required.

W.2884—583. 30,000 Pads—8/14. S. B. Ltd.—Forms/C.2123.

"C" Form (Original). Army Form C. 2123.

MESSAGES AND SIGNALS. No. of Message

Prefix Code Words	Received	Sent, or sent out	Office Stamp.
£ s. d. Charges to collect	From By	At m. To By	30.
Service Instructions.			

Handed in at Extracts – Copy 1 Office m. Received m.

TO: 10th Bde – Som. L.I. – HANTS – LAN. FUS – MONMOUTHS – A & S HIGH – R.I. FUS – ESSEX – ROY. IRISH – R.B. – E LANCS – 11th Bde & SEAFORTHS –

*Sender's Number	Day of Month	In reply to Number	AAA
BM. 664	16th May		

R.B. relieve Som L.I. or HANTS which Battn to be notified later. SEAFORTHS relieve MONS in SHELL TRAP FM & Southwards. Two Coys DUBLINS occupy retrenchment vacated by SEAFORTHS S.W of SHELL TRAP FM. DUBLINS less 2 Coys occupy Div. Support line South of road in C21d road exclusive, relieving ESSEX. WARWICKS relieve Roy IR. FUS in C29a leaving 1 Coy in Div Support line S of ST JEAN – FORTUIN Rd. On relief. Som. L.I. or HANTS to 4th Div Support line N of road C21d road inclusive which will have been vacated by L.R.B. MONMOUTHS ESSEX & Roy IR. to West of CANAL place to be notified later. Roy IR. Fus to LA BRIQUE. LRB to East bank of CANAL North of No 2 PONTOON. – No more Som L.I. or HANTS – LAN. FUS – A & S. Highrs – E LANCS.

FROM

PLACE & TIME

* This line should be erased if not required.

W.2384—583. 80,000 Pads—3/14. S. B. Ltd.—Forms/C.2123.

"C" Form (Original). Army Form C. 2123.

MESSAGES AND SIGNALS. No. of Message

Prefix Code Words

Received From By

Sent, or sent out At m. To By

Office Stamp.

£ s. d.

Charges to collect

Service Instructions.

31

Handed in at URGENT COPY Office m. Received m.

TO L.R.B.

*Sender's Number	Day of Month	In reply to Number	AAA
BM 50	19 May		

Orders	have	just	been	received
that	your	Battn	is	to
be	withdrawn	from	the	4th
Division	tonight	and	sent	to
TATINGHEM	4	miles	west	of
ST OMER	and	should	be	prepared
to	march	at	short	notice

FROM 11th Inf Bde

PLACE & TIME 4.55pm

* This line should be erased if not required.

W.2884—583. 80,000 Pads—8/14. S. B. Ltd.—Forms/C.2123.

"C" Form (Original). Army Form C. 2123.

MESSAGES AND SIGNALS. No. of Message

Prefix / Code / Words	Received	Sent, or sent out	Office Stamp.
Charges to collect £ s. d.	From	At m.	32
Service Instructions.	By	To	
		By	

Handed in at COPY Office m. Received m.

TO L.R.B (1)

*Sender's Number	Day of Month	In reply to Number	AAA
BM 52	19 May		

Following	just	received	AAA	5
Corps	wires	that	LRB	will
forward	tomorrow	20th inst	to	TATINGHEM
where	they	will	~~be~~ pass	under
GOC	GHQ	Troops	AAA	Buses
will	be	sent	to	just
West	of	VLAMERTINGHE	at	9 AM
AAA	LRB	will	march	tonight
to	buildings	in	H3a 5·8	AAA
Advanced	party	should	report	to
Div.	HQ	this	afternoon	AAA
Retain	their	machine	guns	if
serviceable	for	distribution	to	other
units	AAA	Brigade	Transport	Officer
has	already	been	instructed	to
Send	their	transport	to	TATINGHEM
Supply	wagons	Carrying	rations	for

FROM

PLACE & TIME

* This line should be erased if not required.

W.3884—523. 80,000 Pads—3/14. S. B. Ltd.—Forms/C.2123.

"C" Form (Original). Army Form C. 2123.

MESSAGES AND SIGNALS. No. of Message........

Prefix........ Code........ Words........	Received	Sent, or sent out	Office Stamp.
£ s. d.	From........	At........m.	32
Charges to collect	By........	To........	
Service Instructions.		By........	

Handed in at........Office........m. Received........m.

TO (2)

*Sender's Number	Day of Month	In reply to Number	AAA
BM 52	19		

21st	AAA	Rations	for	tomorrow
are	being	delivered	here	and
some	transport	being	sent	on
to	the	Battn	to	bring
their	stores	here.		

FROM 11th Infantry Brigade

PLACE & TIME 5.50 pm

* This line should be erased if not required.

W.2334—583. 30,000 Pads—8/14. S. B. Ltd.—Forms/C.2123.

33

19.5.15

The Officer Commanding 1st Bn LONDON RIFLE BRIGADE.

The Brigadier General Commanding the 11th Infantry Brigade has just learnt that the London Rifle Brigade are leaving his Command tonight.

He deeply regrets that he has therefore no opportunity of personally taking farewell of all ranks of a Battalion which has, for the past 6 months, made a reputation for itself which for courage steadfastness, and devotion to duty, is second to none in the Expeditionary Force.

He and all ranks of the Brigade wish them a good time of rest and recuperation after their very trying experience in the late fighting and hope before long they may be back again among their old comrades of the 11th Infantry Brigade.

Please communicate to all ranks

Signed C. B. PROWSE Brig Genl
Comdg 11th Inf Bde

(1)

Organisation of Composite Battn London Regiment & relief of 6th Battn Welsh Regt on Lines of Communication. (34)

1. O.C. Composite Battn will arrange for the instructions contained in attached paper to be carried out forthwith, & will relieve 6th Battn WELSH. Regmt on May 31. taking over Caserne d'Albret on that date & relieving all 6th Battn WELSH Regmt detachments.

2. He will at once get into touch with O.C. 6th WELSH. Regmt & obtain all necessary information as to duties on Lines of Communication from that officer.

3. Instructions as to railway moves necessary for carrying out 1. above will be issued by D.A.D.R.T. ST OMER station.

4. On relief 6th Battn WELSH Regmt will concentrate at WIZERNES for training on the 1st June.

G.H.Q. 27.5 1915.

(2)

34

Organisation Composite Battalion London Regiment.

Staff.	C.O. Major H.J. Stafford 13th London.
	Adjutant Lt. C. Howard " "
	Remainder of 13th London Regmt Staff.
Composition of Battn.	1/5th Bn London Regmt. (L.R.B)
	1/12th. do. (Rangers)
	1/13. do (Kensingtons)

O.C 1/13th London Regmt. will command the composite Battn as a whole & instructions from superior authority will come through him. Each of 3 units above is to be organised on a 2 Company basis, all the personnel except 2nd line transport drivers being temporary retained.

Distribution of Battn on L. of C.	H.Q. Composite Batt. ST OMER
	H.Q. ∅ 1/5th London Regt. do.
	H.Q. ✗ 1/13. do. do.
	∅. Finds SOUTHERN Railhead
	✗ " NORTHERN do.
	H.Q. 1/12 London Regmt. ETAPLES & CALAIS.
Reinforcements.	All reinforcements to join H.Q. of own unit, not to be utilized as a

general reinforcement for the Composite Battalion as a whole. (3) (34)

<u>Transport.</u> 13th London retains its transport as a whole. Remainder to be handed in by arrangement with DADS&T. GHQ Troops 1st Line drivers to be retained.

<u>Machine Guns.</u> To be handed in through A.O.D. at G.H.Q. railhead.

<u>Handing in Equipment etc.</u> To be arranged with D.A.D.O.S. GHQ Troops at once. Q.M. of Composite Battn. to call at the Office at once.

List of Southern Railheads & Distribution of Troops on L. of C. attached.

(4)

34

List of Southern Railheads
and
Distribution of Troops on L. of C.

Co	Railheads	Places	Officer	O.R.
No 1.	Rest Camp	THEROUANNE.	Q.M.S.	6
	Detraining Stn. N.R.H.	LUMBRES	-	18
	" "	ARQUES.	-	9.
	" "	WIZERNES.	-	9.
No 2.	4th Corps.	LA GORGUE.	1	18.
	Hd. Division	MERVEILLE	-	13.
	Canadian Divn	THIENNES.	1	13.
	1st Army Ammn. O.Z.	ST VENANT.	1	21.
No 3.	1st Corps	CHOCQUES.	1	18.
	Indian Corps	LILLERS.	1	18.
	1st Army Ammn. O.X.	FOUQUEREUIL.	-	21.
	D.R.S.	BETHUNE.	-	13.
4.	Indian Cav. Corps	AIRE.	1	18.
	D.R.S.	BERQUETTE	-	13.
	Ammn. Train	"	-	13
	No 7. R.E. Park	"	-	21.
H.Q. Details	G.H.Q.	ST. OMER.	10.	113.

Casualties May 1915.

Appendix 35

CASUALTIES MAY.

Date	Killed in Action	Killed (continued)	Wounded — Names of officers, Numbers of other ranks
MAY 2.	385 Sgt ROLFE C.	66 Cpl BOOTH A.M.	
	199 L/Cpl HAMPTON J.L.	1139 Pte COOK C.H.	CAPT & HON MAJOR. C.D. BURNELL
	291 Pte NORTHAM J.P.	9937 " GARROD S.E.	" LARGE E.L. – died of wounds, 21/5/15.
	887 " ALLISON W.G.	964 " HIGGINS T.R.	LIEUT. CHARLES D.S.
	674 " JONES W.L.	9547 " JARVIS H.S.	" CARTWRIGHT G.H.G.M.
	809 " KIRKWOOD J.	1065 " LAMB H.	2nd LT WHITE A.B.
	314 " HASELDINE N.W.	228 " BURDGE L.G.	2nd LT. FLINDT R.E.H.
	898 " VALENTINE H.D.	62 " PARR P.G.	2nd LT WIMBLE A.S.
	7183 Coy.S.M. FRANK G.L.	17 Cpl. WIMBLE H.R.	2nd LT. SEDGEWICK A.E.
	8223 Sgt RING. M.J.	9973 Pte BOND T.M.	
	8396 " FEATHERSTONEHAUGH A.P.	617 " HEWITT T.A.	120 other ranks.
	160 Pte BARTLETT	9432 " MOORE R.H.T.	
	1063 " LIGHT J.	976 " WARREN A.L.	
	790 " GUMPRECHT E.H.	9399 " BALDWIN E.W.	
	802 " KERRY H.	9472 " COLEMAN J.N.	
	171 " BUTLER E.	9557 " FAIRS E.W.	
	321 " SMITH W.P.	157 TEAKLE L.H.	
	9576 " KIRK W.H.	9787 L/Cpl JENKINS. C.	
	995 " KILLIP W.	686 Pte WYNN J.F.	
	9730 " DIXON H.S.	9270 " KELSEY S.G.	
	90 " REYNOLDS J.	609 " MATTHEWS P.A.	
	8639 " LONG W.M.	72 " COLEBROOK L.J.	
		9150 " LEGG S.C.	
MAY. 3.	LIEUT. H. B. PRICE	—	Reported Missing
	2nd LT R. LINTOTT		356 Pte LOUCH H. – later reported Prisoner of war 24/5/15
			374 " PILKINGTON. E " " " "
			9588 " ROSE H.G. " " " 29/5/15
			446 " SOUTHALL A.B. later reported Prisoner of war
			745 " HARVEY A.S. " " WOUNDED. at Base
			547 " MAYHEAD C
" 6.	9878 Pte R.W. OFFIN (died in hospital)		

Army Form C. 2118.

WAR DIARY
~~INTELLIGENCE SUMMARY~~
(Erase heading not required.)

Instructions regarding War Diaries and Intelligence Summaries are contained in F. S. Regs. Part II. and the Staff Manual respectively. Title pages will be prepared in manuscript.

Appendix 35

Casualties May 1915. (Contd)

Date	Killed in action	Killed (continued)	Wounded. Officers by name, others ranks by Numbers.
MAY. 9th.	-	-	1 man wounded
" 10 "	9467 Pte W.H. DIXON died in hospital grounds.		
" 12 "	-	-	
" 13th.	2nd LT S.M. LINES	9460 Pte V.A. WOOD	1 man wounded.
	2nd LT. HRW GOODING	350 " E.D. SCHAEFFER	CAPT. R.H. HUSEY
	316. Cpl. AA CLARIDGE	256 " P.R. HOAD	" + ADJT A.C. OPPENHEIM
	370 " F.L. BANKS	9345 L/Cpl E. PARKER	2nd LT. B. E. POCOCK. (Missing)
	9411 L/Cpl. E.G. PAXTON	614 Cpl. L. HAWKINS	2nd LT. A.W.T. BETTS
	9575 " W.S. CLARIDGE	1201 Pte G.N. FREEMAN	+ 49 other ranks.
	9721 " R.G. CANNELL	335 " J.W. PREBBLE	
	9887 " B.H. RICHARDSON	495 " T.H. MADLEY	MISSING
	768 Pte G. TOWNSEND	9365 " W.F. GALPIN	298 Pte. HODGSON. W.
	9555 " C.A.M. PIPER	395 " F. SIDNELL	831 " BROUGHTON W.C.
	779 " J.R. WAGSTAFF	9903 Sgt. H. COULSON	332 " BEESTON H.L.
	313 " C.S. POWIS	8380 L/Cpl. F.E. SPARKS	
	777 " P. BATES	233 " V.R. BROWN	
	9220 Sgt. W.P.S. MARSHALL	579 Pte S.T. LUND	
	9295 Cpl. E.C.D. SLOW	131 " L.D. LLOYD	
	222 Pte P. McELWEE	9444 " J.W. DAWSON	
	9409 " J.V. MARSH		
	1077 " L.F. BARTLETT		
	9505 " F.H. COLE		
" 14th.	9590 L/Cpl A.C. DAY	735 Pte J.W. SODEN - died in Hospital grounds	3 men wounded.
15th.	304 Pte S.J. CONDUIT died in hospital grounds	-	5 men wounded
	9330 " H.M.P. VAN KOERT " "		

GHQ Troops

4th Division

121/5935.

1/5th London Regt (L.R.B.)

Vol VIII 1—30.6.15

Army Form C. 2118.

Instructions regarding War Diaries and Intelligence Summaries are contained in F. S. Regs., Part II. and the Staff Manual respectively. Title pages will be prepared in manuscript.

WAR DIARY
or
~~INTELLIGENCE SUMMARY~~

(*Erase heading not required.*)

Hour, Date, Place		Summary of Events and Information	Remarks and references to Appendices
June 1 Tatinghen.	8 AM	Headquarters & remainder of Battn moved to St. Omer. & quartered in French Artillery Barracks. - Caserne d'Albret. - under command of Major H. J. Stafford. O.C. Composite Battn.	
	9 AM	Arrived St. Omer. in Barracks. Officers billeted in town. Transport entrained & sent to Abbeville in charge of Sergt Peerless & 75 men.	
" 2. St. Omer.	2 pm	6th Welsh Regmt marched out of Barracks. to Wizernes. General fatigues cleaning up Barracks which were left in dirty state.	
		Telegram sent to Queen Victoria's Rifles congratulating them on the occasion of V.C. awarded to one of their officers. & received the attached reply.	vide Appendix No 36.
" 3. "		L.R.B. Details paraded & drilled by the following newly appointed officers. 2/Lt. Barker. 2/Lt. Crews. 2/Lt. Boston.	
		Letter received from Bishop of London. vide copy attached	Appendix No 37.
" 4 "		New L.R.B Badges recived & issued to all N.C.O. & men. C.O. inspected kits of all men in Barracks & the new Badges sewn on Serge tunics.	

1247 W 3299 200,000 (E) 8/14 J.B.C. & A. Forms/C. 2118/11.

Instructions regarding War Diaries and Intelligence Summaries are contained in F. S. Regs., Part II. and the Staff Manual respectively. Title pages will be prepared in manuscript.

WAR DIARY
or
~~INTELLIGENCE~~ SUMMARY
(Erase heading not required.)

Army Form C. 2118.

Hour, Date, Place	Summary of Events and Information	Remarks and references to Appendices
June 5. ST OMER.	Detachments at LUMBRES and WIZERNES return to H.Q.	
9 PM.	Sergt PEARLESS & 15 men return from ABBEVILLE having returned Transport to Advance Base.	
" 6. Do. 10.45.	Church Parade in Soldiers Club Room near Barracks. News that Leave granted to all ranks who came out with Battalion & had had no leave. – Officers 7 days. NCO & men 72 hours. –	
2 pm.	Major Bates granted 18 days leave & left for ENGLAND. Captain A. L. LINTOTT took over command of Battalion. 87. N.C.O. & men rejoined from Base Depot Camp @ HARVE. 2nd Lt. BARKER & 2/Lt. CREWS left for Leave.	
" 7. Do.	General fatigues & Guards. Very hot. 12 N.C.O. left for leave.	. 1 case German Measles reported & sent Hospital. –
" 8 Do.	Rejoined men inspected & clothing renewed. 18 N.C.O. & men rejoined from Base Depot Camp.	
" 9. Do.	Fine & very hot. Physical Drill, General Fatigues & Guards. No. of N.C.O. & men for leave each day increased from 12. to 24. Thunder storm in afternoon.	
" 10 Do.	Fine & cooler. Draft of 50 men arrived from ENGLAND. Detachment from FOQUEREUIL returned " RE. Nº7. Park @ BERGUETTE. returned.	

1247 W 3299 200,000 (E) 8/14 J.B.C. & A. Forms/C. 2118/11.

Instructions regarding War Diaries and Intelligence Summaries are contained in F. S. Regs., Part II. and the Staff Manual respectively. Title pages will be prepared in manuscript.

WAR DIARY
or
~~INTELLIGENCE SUMMARY.~~
(Erase heading not required.)

Army Form C. 2118.

Hour, Date, Place	Summary of Events and Information	Remarks and references to Appendices
June 11 St OMER.	Fine. Physical Drill. General Fatigues & Guards. Letter received from 4th Division Maj-General WILSON stating that the "Behaviour of the Regiment in the operations EAST of YPRÉS was most gallant & praiseworthy". Copy	vide Appendix No. 38.
" 12 Do.	Fine. Physical Drill. General Fatigues & Guards.	
" 13 Do	" Church Parade 10.45. Service in "Soldiers Club Room"	
" 14 Do.	" Physical Drill. General Fatigues & Guards. Received letter from 4th Division stating that C-in-C. had awarded the D.C.M. to the following N.C.Os. No. 9338. Sergt. W.F. POTHECARY. No. 75. L/Corpl T.H. STRANSON.	
" 15 Do.	Fine. Physical Drill. General Fatigues & Guards.	
" 16 Do	" " " " " "	
" 17. Do.	" " " " " " Draft men practised in Rapid & Grouping Practices on Range Loan of Machine Gun for Instructional purposes from M.G. School	
" 18. Do.	Fine. Physical Drill General Fatigues & Guards. Draft men despatched to their respective Companies.	

Instructions regarding War Diaries and Intelligence Summaries are contained in F. S. Regs., Part II. and the Staff Manual respectively. Title pages will be prepared in manuscript.

WAR DIARY
or
~~INTELLIGENCE SUMMARY.~~

(Erase heading not required.)

Army Form C. 2118.

Hour, Date, Place	Summary of Events and Information	Remarks and references to Appendices
June 19. ST OMER.	Holy Communion Service held @ 6.30 in Soldiers Club in connection with Regimental Memorial Service being held by Bishop of London in London. Nearly all N.C.O. & men available in Barracks attended. Physical Drill. General Fatigues & Guards. 10. German Prisoners arrived under escort.	
" 20 Do.	Church Parade @ 10.45. in Soldiers Club Room.	
" 21. Do.	Fine. Physical Drill 6.15AM Inspection of Rifles & Drill 9.50 AM General Fatigues & Guards.	
" 22 Do.	Fine. General Fatigues Guards. & Physical Drill. 7. N.C.O & men. to Maxim Gun School to be trained as Instructors.	
" 23. Do.	Fine. Physical Drill 6.15 AM. General Fatigues & Guards. Sergt. R.V. TODD (No 8541). awarded D.C.M. Major A.S. BATES & Capt. R.H. HUSEY mentioned in Despatches.	
" 24 Do.	Fine. Physical Drill 6.15AM. General Fatigues & Guards. & Pitching Camp for Battalion. Honours List. Major A.S. BATES. awarded D.S.O. Capt. R.H. HUSEY " Military Cross Sergt. D.W. BELCHER " VICTORIA CROSS.	– vide Appendix No. 39. & 39A

(73989) W4141—463. 400,000. 9/14. H.&J.Ltd. Forms/C. 2118/10.

Instructions regarding War Diaries and Intelligence Summaries are contained in F. S. Regs., Part II. and the Staff Manual respectively. Title pages will be prepared in manuscript.

WAR DIARY
or
~~INTELLIGENCE SUMMARY.~~ Ahh
(Erase heading not required.)

Army Form C. 2118.

Hour, Date, Place	Summary of Events and Information	Remarks and references to Appendices
June 24th (continued) 8.20 pm	Major A.S. BATES. D.S.O. returned from Leave in England & took over command of Battalion.	
" 25. ST. OMER.	Fine. Physical Drill, Guards & General Fatigues. Major BATES saw the Adjutant-General @ G.H.Q. The C.O. Composite London Battn (Major STAFFORD) left & Major Bates takes over command of Composite Battn.	
" 26 "	Rained during morning. Physical Drill Guards & General Fatigues.	
" 27 "	Fine. Church Parade @ 10.45 AM Small parade owing to number of men for Fatigues & Duty.	
" 28 "	Showery. Guards & General Fatigues. 17. Riflemen returned from BASE Depot Rouen. Wire received from 4th Division stating that Military Cross had been awarded to LIEUT. C.W. TREVELYAN.	
" 29 "	Fine. Physical Drill, Guards & General Fatigues. Preparation to move into Camp tomorrow.	
30 "	Fine. Moved into Camp on ground adjoining Infantry Barracks @ 11.30. General Fatigues & Guards. Deputy Inspector General of Lines of Communication visited the Camp @ 3. o'clock. Lieut. C.W. Trevelyan returned from leave @ 8.pm.	

(73989) W4141—463. 400,000. 9/14. H.&J.Ltd. Forms/C. 2118/10.

36

Copy of letter
From O.C. Queen Victoria's Rifles
To O.C. London Rifle Brigade

The O.C. Queen Victoria's Rifles on behalf of the Officers, N.C.O's & Riflemen of the Regiment, begs to thank the Officers, N.C.O's & Riflemen of the London Rifle Brigade for their wire conveying their congratulations on the occasion of Lieut. Woolley being awarded the V.C.

The Q.V.R's send the best of wishes & good luck to the L.R.B. & hope to be able to send a similar wire to you soon.

(37)

The following letter has been received from the Bishop of London and is published for information.

"I want to write to you, as representing the Regiment to say how deeply proud I am of them all for the splendid way they have behaved.

I read the account in the Times with pride but I am deeply grieved at the loss of so many gallant comrades."

(38)

Copy of Letter

G.O.C, G.H.Q Troops

I have much pleasure in informing you that the G.O.C 11th Infantry Brigade has referred in the following terms to the action of the London Rifle Brigade, during the operations East of YPRES from the 9th to the 13th May.—

"The Behaviour of this Battalion was most gallant & praiseworthy"

"It stuck to its trenches under heavy shell fire, and was always dependable and ready for anything"

Sd/ H F M Wilson
Maj.-General
Commdg. 4th Div.

6th June 1915

Extract from Battalion Orders 25th June 1915

Victoria Cross

The Commanding Officer wishes to congratulate Sgt Belcher on the most distinguished honour he, and the Battalion, has received by the award of the Victoria Cross for his gallant conduct on May 13th

The following N.C.O's & Riflemen were with Sgt Belcher on this occasion:-

9471	L/Corpl	ROWE	H.J	
9828	do	WHEATLEY	J.H	Wounded
1124	Rfm	BUCK	H.G	do
9399	do	EVANS	C.M.	
1201	do	FREEMAN	G.W	Killed
304	do	PARKER	H	
9485	do	ROWE	H.W.	
9624	do	WEEKS	R.S.	Wounded

(39)

Copy of Extract from "The Times"

London Gazette. Honours. dated Thursday June 24th 1915

No. 9539 Lance-Sergeant DOUGLAS WALTER BELCHER 1-5th (City of London) Battalion, the London Regiment (London Rifle Brigade)

"On the early morning of May 13th 1915 when in charge of a portion of an advanced breastwork, south of the WIELTJE - ST. JULIEN Road during a very fierce and continuous bombardment by the enemy, which frequently blew in the breastwork, Lance-Sergeant BELCHER with a mere handful of men elected to remain and endeavour to hold his position after the troops near him had been withdrawn. By his skill & great gallantry he maintained his position during the day, opening rapid fire on the enemy, who were only 150 to 200 yards distant, whenever he saw them collecting for an attack. There is little doubt that the bold front shown by Lance Sergeant BELCHER prevented the enemy breaking through on the WIELTJE Road, and averted an attack on the flank of one of our divisions."

GHQ Troops

11/XX

4th Division

121/6390

5th London (L.R. Bde).

Vol IX

1 - 31 - 4 - 15

Nil

Instructions regarding War Diaries and Intelligence Summaries are contained in F. S. Regs., Part II. and the Staff Manual respectively. Title pages will be prepared in manuscript.

WAR DIARY
or
INTELLIGENCE SUMMARY.
(Erase heading not required.)

Army Form C. 2118.

Hour, Date, Place	Summary of Events and Information	Remarks and references to Appendices
July 1st Camp ST OMER	Fine. 6.15AM. Physical Drill. General Fatigues & Guards	
2 " D^o.	Fine & Hot 6.15AM. Physical Drill. 9.AM. Company Drill for NCOs & men not on duty. General Fatigues & Guards. Signallers & Maxim Gun teams start training under respective Instructors.	
3. " "	Fine & Hot 6.15AM. Physical Drill. Company Drill. General Fatigues & Guards. Lt Johnston (Acting Adjutant) 2/Lt. RUSSELL, & 2/Lt. CHARLES, go on leave. Lt JOHNSTON & Lt. TREVELYAN promoted Tempy Captains. (vide London Gazette 2.7.1915)	
4 " D^o.	Fine. Cooler. 10.45. Church Parade in Soldier's Club for those not on duty. General Fatigues & Guards. Captain. A.L. LINTOTT takes over the duties of A/Adjutant. Received letter from Queen Victoria Rifles congratulating L/Sergt BELCHER & the Regiment on his being awarded the "Victoria Cross".	
5 " D^o.	Fine 6.15AM. Physical Drill. Company Drill & Inspection of Rifles. General Fatigues & Guards. Sergt BELCHER. V.C. returns to H.Q. from Railhead. STATION. MERVILLE.	
6 " D^o.	Fine 6.15AM Physical Drill. Drill. General Fatigues & Guards. Instruction to NCOs & men in putting up barbed wire.	HSJ

Instructions regarding War Diaries and Intelligence Summaries are contained in F. S. Regs., Part II. and the Staff Manual respectively. Title pages will be prepared in manuscript.

WAR DIARY
or
INTELLIGENCE SUMMARY.
(Erase heading not required.)

Army Form C. 2118.

Hour, Date, Place	Summary of Events and Information	Remarks and references to Appendices
July 6 (continued)	entanglements under 2/Lt Maynard. Major Bate D.S.O. Captain TREVELYAN (Military Cross) L/Sergt BELCHER V.C left for England on special leave to have Decorations awarded to them presented them by H.M. THE KING.	
July 7 In camp ST OMER	Fine & showery. 6.15 AM Physical Drill. Company Drill & Musketry. General fatigues & Guards. Instruction Wire Entanglements.	
" 8 " "	Fine. Do. Do.	
" 9 " "	Fine & overcast. Cooler. Do. Do.	
" 10 " "	Fine - Heavy Storm in afternoon, several tents flooded out. 6.15 AM Physical Drill. Detraining Detachments wanted at AUBRICQ & WATTEN for Detraining the "RADDISH" Division. General fatigues & Guards. Practically no men in camp. SEC LIEUT'S to be Temp LIEUT.S F.H. WALLIS (May 3). R. RUSSELL (June 11)	to London Gazette 9/7/15.
" 11 " "	Fine. Wind dried up the Camp. 10.45 Church parade SOLDIER'S CLUB. 2/Lt F. S. CHARLES returned from leave. 2Lt S.R. HOGGE rejoined from Hospital.	
" 12 " "	Fine. All N.C.O. & men on duty. General fatigues & guards. Captain OTTER - LT. WALLIS go on leave. 2/Lt CHARLES returns to Railhead LILLERS.	HH

(73989) W4141-463. 400,000. 9/14. H.&J.Ltd. Forms/C. 2118/10.

Instructions regarding War Diaries and Intelligence Summaries are contained in F. S. Regs., Part II. and the Staff Manual respectively. Title pages will be prepared in manuscript.

WAR DIARY
or
INTELLIGENCE SUMMARY.
(Erase heading not required.)

Army Form C. 2118.

Hour, Date, Place	Summary of Events and Information	Remarks and references to Appendices
July 12. (continued).	The following receive decorations & orders from H.M. THE KING at Buckingham Palace. Major. Bates. D.S.O. Cpt. TREVELYAN. Military Cross. Sergt. BELCHER VICTORIA CROSS.	
" 13. In camp ST. OMER.	Fine. General fatigues & Guards. Detachments for detraining moved from AUDRUICQ & WATTEN. to WIZERNES. & LUMBRES. for detraining New Divisions. Detraining party also sent to ARQUES. Capt LINTOTT. visited detachments at all Railheads up to BETHUNE.	
" 14. " "	Fine. General fatigues & Guards. 5 cases of Guava Jelly received from Lord Mayor of LONDON. for distribution. & a number of SUN FLAPS from The BEE BADMINGTON CLUB.	
" 15 " "	Fine. Major BATES. D.S.O. & Capt. TREVELYAN returned from leave. General fatigues & Guards.	
" 16 " "	Showery. General fatigues & Guards. Lt RUSSELL & 60 men	
" 17 " "	" Guards. proceeded to BETHUNE.	H.H.
	Major A S BATES. DSO. promoted Temp. Lt.-Colonel 16th April.	vide London Gazette. 15/7/15

(73989) W4141—463. 400,000. 9/14. H.&J.Ltd. Forms/C. 2118/10.

Instructions regarding War Diaries and Intelligence Summaries are contained in F. S. Regs., Part II. and the Staff Manual respectively. Title pages will be prepared in manuscript.

WAR DIARY
or
INTELLIGENCE SUMMARY.
(Erase heading not required.)

Army Form C. 2118.

Hour, Date, Place	Summary of Events and Information	Remarks and references to Appendices
July 18. In camp. ST OMER.	Fine. Capt. TREVELYAN with 1 officer of KENSINGTON's, 3 officers RANGERS & 150 NCO & men of RANGERS proceeded to unknown destination as H.Q. Troops to New III ARMY.	
	Capt. JOHNSTON A/ADJUTANT returned from leave.	
	Details in camp paraded with ARTIST'S RIFLES for Church	
" 19 " "	Fine. Guards & fatigues with the few men left in camp.	
	Rfn 239 BAYLIS. R.W. Severely injured while detraining wagons.	
" 20 " "	Fatigues & guards as usual.	
" 21 " "	" " " "	
" 22 " "	" " " " Sgt EDMUNDS joined from base to complete records	
" 23 " "	" " " "	
" 24 " "	" " " "	
" 25 " "	" " " " All leave stopped for N.C.O's & men	
	Lt de COLOGAN. A.T.B. " CHOLMELEY. G.H. " FURSDON. G.E.S. 2nd Lt BRODIE C.G. WHITE. A.B APPLETON. E.R. ASTE. P.J. } Joined from England for duty.	HJ

(73989) W4141—463. 400,000. 9/14. H.&J.Ltd. Forms/C. 2118/10.

Army Form C. 2118.

Instructions regarding War Diaries and Intelligence Summaries are contained in F. S. Regs., Part II. and the Staff Manual respectively. Title pages will be prepared in manuscript.

WAR DIARY
or
INTELLIGENCE SUMMARY.
(Erase heading not required.)

Hour, Date, Place	Summary of Events and Information	Remarks and references to Appendices
July 26th Camp St OMER.	Guards & Fatigues as usual 2nd Lt POGOSE E.R., ROSE. E.W. } Joined from England.	
" 27 " "	" " " " 9088 Lcpl. CREGOE. J.P., 9137 – STONNILL R.H., 9385 Rfn ASHBY. H.H., 803 – CATCHSIDE. E.E., 9646 COLE H.G., 9584 CROSS P.F., 9638 MILLAR W.W., 337 STEELE. W.C., 587 WOULDHAM. A.W. } Join the Officers School at BLENDECQUES as Cadets.	
11-45 P.M.	Hostile aeroplane dropped 6 bombs on the Town.	
" " 28 Camp St OMER	Guards & fatigues as usual.	
" 29 " "	" " " " Capt LINTOTT & 2nd Lt OLDFIELD returned from leave.	
" " " 7.15 AM	Aeroplane over Town one bomb dropped slightly wounding one LRB man.	
4.30 P.M.	Capt LINTOTT accident while riding taken to Hospital concussed.	
" 30 Camp St Omer	8. AM Another aeroplane over but driven off without dropping any bombs. Guards & Fatigues as usual.	
July 31st " "	" " " " "	

H.H.

(73989) W4141—463. 400,000. 9/14. H.&J.Ltd. Forms/C. 2118/10.

G.H.Q.

121
6587

5th London (Rifle Brig) Regt.

Vol X

From 1 - 31. 8. 15

[illegible]

Confidential

WAR. DIARY

London Rifle Brigade

1st August. 1915 to. 31st August.

Instructions regarding War Diaries and Intelligence Summaries are contained in F. S. Regs., Part II. and the Staff Manual respectively. Title pages will be prepared in manuscript.

WAR DIARY
or
INTELLIGENCE SUMMARY.
(Erase heading not required.)

Army Form C. 2118.

Hour, Date, Place	Summary of Events and Information	Remarks and references to Appendices
Aug. 1st Camp ST. OMER	Guards, fatigues, & duties as usual.	CH.7.1.
2	" " " "	
3	" " " "	
4 " "	Guards, fatigues, & duties as usual. Capt. C.H.F. THOMPSON rejoined from ENGLAND for duty & took over the duties of Second in Command from Capt. A.L. LINTOTT.	
5. " "	Guards, fatigues, & duties as usual	
6. " "	" " "	
7. " "	" " "	
8.	Lt. de COLOSAN, A.T.B. } 2nd Lt. WHITE, A.B. } " ASTE, P.J. } attended for a Course at the Machine Gun School, G.H.Q.	
	Extract from LONDON Gazette _ Capt. (Temp. Lieut. Col.) A.S. BATES, D.S.O. to be Major (dated 6 March 1915)	

Instructions regarding War Diaries and Intelligence Summaries are contained in F. S. Regs., Part II. and the Staff Manual respectively. Title pages will be prepared in manuscript.

WAR DIARY
or
INTELLIGENCE SUMMARY.
(Erase heading not required.)

Army Form C. 2118.

Hour, Date, Place	Summary of Events and Information	Remarks and references to Appendices
Aug. 9th. In Camp ST OMER	Guards, Fatigues, & duties as usual.	(H.7.T.)
	Lt. HARNEY, B.S. rejoined for duty from ENGLAND	
	2nd Lt. DODDS, A.K. " " — " HAVRE.	
" 10 " —	Guards, Fatigues, & duties as usual.	ROUTINE ORDERS by
" 11 " —	The Battalion resumed its individual formation from this date. vide Appendix.	Lieut. General Sir F. T. CLAYTON, K.C.M.G. C.B.
	Guards, Fatigues, & duties as usual.	
" 12 " " "	Guards, Fatigues, & duties as usual.	I. G. C. 9th Aug. 1915.
" 13 " " "	" do. " do.	223. Composite Battalion, the LONDON Regt. – Formations
	Capt. A.L. LINDOTT returned to duty from Hospital.	The 5th, 12th, and 13th Battalions of the LONDON Regiment, at present forming the Composite Battalion, will resume their individual formations from this date.
	Capt. & Adjt. H.L. JOHNSTON admitted to Hospital.	
	Capt. C.W. TREVELYAN took over the duties of Adjutant vice Capt. JOHNSTON.	
" 14 " —	Guards, Fatigues, & duties as usual.	
" 15 —	do — do —	

(73989) W4141—463. 400,000. 9/14. H.&J.Ltd. Forms/C. 2118/10.

Instructions regarding War Diaries and Intelligence Summaries are contained in F. S. Regs., Part II. and the Staff Manual respectively. Title pages will be prepared in manuscript.

WAR DIARY
or
INTELLIGENCE SUMMARY.
(Erase heading not required.)

Army Form C. 2118.

Hour, Date, Place	Summary of Events and Information	Remarks and references to Appendices
Aug. 16th. in Camp ST OMER.	Guards, Fatigues, & duties as usual.	
" 17. —— "	do —— do.	CH.7.7.
" 18. —— "	Capt. R.E. OTTER reported for duty from ENGLAND.	
	One N.C.O & three Riflemen proceeded to the Cadet School at BLENDECQUES for a course of instruction.	
	Guards, Fatigues, & duties as usual.	
" 19 —— "	Capt. C.H.F. THOMPSON, " A.L. LINTOTT, " R.E. OTTER, 2nd Lieut. T.D. CHARLES, " E.W. ROSE, " C.G. BRODIE } attended a course of instruction in "Bombing", conducted by Capt. WYATT, 29th Coy. R.E. at the Artillery Barracks, ST OMER.	
	Guards, Fatigues, & duties as usual.	
" 20 —— "	All Company Officers attended a course of lectures on "musketry" by Capt. R.E. OTTER in Camp.	
	Guards, Fatigues, & duties as usual.	
	A draft of 2 N.C.Os & 14 Riflemen arrived from the 2nd Batn. LONDON RIFLE BRIGADE in ENGLAND.	

(73989) W4141—463. 400,000. 9/14. H.&J.Ltd. Forms/C. 2118/10.

Instructions regarding War Diaries and Intelligence Summaries are contained in F. S. Regs., Part II. and the Staff Manual respectively. Title pages will be prepared in manuscript.

WAR DIARY
or
INTELLIGENCE SUMMARY.
(Erase heading not required.)

Army Form C. 2118.

Hour, Date, Place	Summary of Events and Information	Remarks and references to Appendices
Aug. 20th In Camp ST OMER	The following Officers were appointed to command	(A17.1.)
	"A" Coy. Capt. C. W. TREVELYAN.	
	"B" " " A. L. LINTOTT.	
	"C" " Lieut. A. T. B. de - COLOGAN.	
	"D" " Capt. R. E. OTTER.	
	Lieut. B. S. HARVEY took over the duties of Machine Gun Officer.	
	Capt. & Adjt. H. L. JOHNSTON returned to duty from Hospital.	
	Guards, Fatigues, & duties as usual.	
" 21 " "	do do.	
" 22 " "	do do.	
" 23 " "	do do.	
" 24 " "	do do.	
" 25 " "	2nd Lieut. A. K. DODDS was detached from the Battalion & proceeded to join 170th Coy R. E. by order of A. A. G. I. G. C. A. B. 6668.	
	Guards, Fatigues, & duties as usual.	
" 26 " "	do do.	

(73989) W4141—463. 400,000. 9/14. H.&J.Ltd. Forms/C. 2118/10.

Instructions regarding War Diaries and Intelligence Summaries are contained in F. S. Regs., Part II. and the Staff Manual respectively. Title pages will be prepared in manuscript.

WAR DIARY
or
INTELLIGENCE SUMMARY.
(Erase heading not required.)

Army Form C. 2118.

Hour, Date, Place	Summary of Events and Information	Remarks and references to Appendices
Aug. 27th In Camp ST OMER	Capt. R.E. OTTER concluded his course of musketry instruction (vide entry for 20th Aug.)	CHT
	Guards, Fatigues, & duties as usual.	
" 28 —	2nd Lieut. F.D. CHARLES attended the Machine-Gun School G.H.Q. for a course of instruction.	
	Guards & duties as usual.	
" 29 —	Guards, Fatigues, & duties as usual.	
" 30 —	do — do.	
" 31 —	do — do.	
	During the month a Machine-Gun instructional class for all Subaltern officers was conducted by Lieut. B.S. HARVEY, the Battalion Machine-Gun Officer.	
	COMMISSIONS. During the month of August 33 N.C.Os & Rfmn left the Battalion in order to take up Commissions in H.M. Regular & Territorial Forces, & 4 N.C.Os & Rfn proceeded to the Cadet School at BLENDECQUES for a course of instruction.	

(73989) W4141—463. 400,000. 9/14. H.&J.Ltd. Forms/C. 2118/10.

11

G. H. Q.

121/7016

CONFIDENTIAL.

WAR DIARY

OF

1/5th London Regt

(LONDON RIFLE BRIGADE)

(1st BATTALION)

FROM. 1st September 1915 To. 30th September 1915

Vol XI

v 20/7016

Instructions regarding War Diaries and Intelligence Summaries are contained in F. S. Regs., Part II. and the Staff Manual respectively. Title pages will be prepared in manuscript.

WAR DIARY
or
INTELLIGENCE SUMMARY.
(Erase heading not required.)

Army Form C. 2118.

Hour, Date, Place	Summary of Events and Information	Remarks and references to Appendices
Sept. 1st In Camp ST OMER	Guards, Fatigues, & duties as usual	CH. ?? Major.
	14 N.C.Os & Riflemen left to attend a course of instruction at the Cadet Training School for Officers at BLENDECQUES.	
Sept. 2nd "	Guards, Fatigues, & duties as usual	
" 3rd	do — do.	
	Capt. R.E. OTTER, Lieut. F.H. WALLIS, 2nd " A.B. WHITE, " " F.D. CHARLES } left to attend a course of instruction with the 187th Coy. R.E.	
" 4th "	Guards, Fatigues, & duties as usual.	
	Lt. G.E.S. FURSDON proceeded to England for duty.	
" 5th "	Guards, Fatigues, & duties as usual.	
" 6th "	do " do.	
	A Draft of 205 N.C.Os & Rfn joined the Battn. from England, were taken on the strength, & posted to Coys. as follows :— A Coy. 53, B " 39, C " 49, D " 64. The following officers were tempy. posted to Coys. as follows:— A. Coy 2nd Lt. P.J. ASTE, B. " C.S. BRODIE, C. " E.W. ROSE, D. " 2nd Lts E.R. APPLETON, J.R. ??	

Instructions regarding War Diaries and Intelligence Summaries are contained in F. S. Regs., Part II. and the Staff Manual respectively. Title pages will be prepared in manuscript.

WAR DIARY
or
INTELLIGENCE SUMMARY.
(Erase heading not required.)

Army Form C. 2118.

Hour, Date, Place	Summary of Events and Information	Remarks and references to Appendices
Sept. 7th In Camp ST OMER	Guards, Fatigues, & duties as usual. Draft at disposal of O.C. Coys for training. Extract from LONDON GAZETTE :- Capt. C.H.T. THOMPSON to be temp. Major d/Aug. 9. 15; Lieut. G.H. CHOLMELEY to be temp. Captain: Lieut. A.T.B. de COLOGAN to be temp. Capt. both dated 9 Aug. 1915.	CHTT. Major
" 8th " " "	Guards, Fatigues, & duties as usual. Draft at disposal of O.C. Coys for training.	
" 9th " "	do " do do " do. 2nd Lt. A.K. DODDS was seconded for duty with 170th Coy. R.E. from 25 Aug. 1915.	
" 10th " "	Guards, Fatigues, & duties as usual. Draft at disposal of O.C. Coys. 20 N.C.Os. & Rfn of the 8th Draft joined the Battn from ROUEN. Extract from LONDON GAZETTE: Lt. B.S. HARVEY to be temp. Captain 9.8.15: 2nd Lt. A.B. WHITE to be temp. Lieut. 29.4.15: 2nd Lt. F.H. CREWS to be temp. Lieut. 30.4.15: 2nd Lt. E.C. WILLS to be temp. Lieut. 3.6.15: 2nd F.D. CHARLES to be temp. Lieut. 3.6.15: 2nd Lieut. M.J. MAYNARD to be temp. Lieut. 7.6.15.	

(73989) W4141—463. 400,000. 9/14. H.&J.Ltd. Forms/C. 2118/10.

Instructions regarding War Diaries and Intelligence Summaries are contained in F. S. Regs., Part II. and the Staff Manual respectively. Title pages will be prepared in manuscript.

WAR DIARY
or
INTELLIGENCE SUMMARY.
(Erase heading not required.)

Army Form C. 2118.

Hour, Date, Place	Summary of Events and Information	Remarks and references to Appendices
Sept. 11th In Camp ST OMER	Guards, Fatigues, & duties as usual.	
" 12th " " "	do. " do. Draft of B. & C. Companies at disposal of O.C. Companies.	CH.F.T. Major
" 13th " " "	Guards, Fatigues, & duties as usual.	
" 14th " " "	do " do.	
" 15th " " "	do " do. The Drafts of all Companies had musketry practice on the Range. Capt. CHOLMELEY & 21 N.C.Os & Rfn proceeded to WIZERNES for duty. 2nd Lieut. C.G. BRODIE was transferred to ENGLAND for duty.	
" 16th " " "	Guards, Fatigues, & duties as usual.	
" 17th " " "	do. " do 19 Rfn were attached to G.H.Q Troop Train for a course of instruction in Transport Duties.	
" 18th " " "	Guards, Fatigues, & duties as usual.	
" 19th " " "	do " do. All Companies had musketry practice on the Range.	

(73989) W4141—463. 400,000. 9/14. H.&J.Ltd. Forms/C. 2118/10.

Army Form C. 2118.

Instructions regarding War Diaries and Intelligence Summaries are contained in F. S. Regs., Part II. and the Staff Manual respectively. Title pages will be prepared in manuscript.

WAR DIARY
or
INTELLIGENCE SUMMARY.

(Erase heading not required.)

Hour, Date, Place	Summary of Events and Information	Remarks and references to Appendices
Sept. 20th In Camp ST OMER	Guards, Fatigues, & duties as usual. Companies at disposal of O.C. Companies.	
" 21st ——— "	do. " do. do ——— " do.	CH7.T. Major.
	2nd Lieut. ROSE & 10 N.C.Os & Rfn proceeded to LILLERS for duty.	
" 22nd ——— "	Guards, Fatigues, & duties as usual. 8 N.C.Os & Rfn proceeded to attend a course of instruction at the Cadet Training School for Officers at BLENDECQUES.	
" 23rd ——— "	Guards, Fatigues, & duties as usual. Companies at disposal of O.C. Coys.	
" 24th ——— "	do ——— do. do ——— " do.	
" 25th " "	do " do. Lieut. RUSSELL & 44 N.C.Os & Rfn proceeded to CHOCQUES to escort prisoners of war.	
" 26th " "	Guards, Fatigues, & duties as usual. Capt. HARVEY & 31 N.C.Os & Rfn proceeded to MERVILLE to escort prisoners of war. Capt. TREVELYAN & 51 N.C.Os & Rfn proceeded to CHOCQUES, & Capt. LINTOTT & 57 N.C.Os & Rfn proceeded to CHOCQUES, in each case to escort prisoners of war.	

(73989) W4141—463. 400,000. 9/14. H.&J.Ltd. Forms/C. 2118/10.

Instructions regarding War Diaries and Intelligence Summaries are contained in F. S. Regs., Part II. and the Staff Manual respectively. Title pages will be prepared in manuscript.

WAR DIARY
or
INTELLIGENCE SUMMARY.
(Erase heading not required.)

Army Form C. 2118.

Hour, Date, Place	Summary of Events and Information	Remarks and references to Appendices
Sept. 27th. In Camp ST. OMER	Guards, & duties as usual.	C.H.-T.T. Major
" 28th " "	" " " Capt. R.E. OTTER, Lieut. F.H. WALLIS, & Lieut. F.D. CHARLES returned to duty with the Battalion. These Officers Commanded sections of "Gas Companies" during the attack delivered by the First Army on the morning of Sept. 25th. Capt. J.G. ROBINSON returned to duty with the Battalion from ROUEN. A draft of 75 N.C.Os & Rfn joined the Battalion from ENGLAND.	
" 29th " "	Guards & duties as usual. Lieut. A.B. WHITE returned from doing duty with a "Gas Company" (see above).	
" 30th " "	do & do. The Draft were engaged in musketry practice on the Range.	
	During the course of the month 22 N.C.Os & Rfn proceeded to ENGLAND to take up commissions in the Regular & Territorial Forces, & 22 N.C.Os & Rfn proceeded on a course of instruction at the Cadet Training School for Officers at BLENDECQUES.	

(73989) W4141—463. 400,000. 9/14. H.&J.Ltd. Forms/C. 2118/10.

"A" Form. Army Form C. 2121.

MESSAGES AND SIGNALS.

No. of Message

Prefix	Code	m.	Words	Charge	This message is on a/c of:	Recd. at m.
Office of Origin and Service Instructions			Sent		WAR DIARY	Date
			At m.		Service.	From
			To			
			By		(Signature of "Franking Officer.")	By

TO { Railsection G.H.Q

Sender's Number	Day of Month	In reply to Number	AAA
* AB.9185	30/9/15		

Q.M.G.	wires	begins	5th	London
Regt	is	to	be	withdrawn
into	G.H.Q	Troops	as	soon
as	possible	aaa	Suggest	your
authorizing	Commandant	No 1	Section	L.O.C.
to	carry	out	transfer	direct
with	G.O.C	G.H.Q	Troops	aaa
Please	inform	me	date	of
transfer	ends	Please	arrange	&
report	aaa	Let	me	know
number	&	disposition	of	your
Troops	at	3rd	Army	Railheads
&	I	will	relieve	them
from	Etaples			

From Communications

Place 7.25.p.m.

Time

Certified true copy
S. Proctor
Staff Capt.

The above may be forwarded as now corrected.

Censor.

(Z)

Signature of Addressor or person authorised to telegraph in his name.

* This line should be erased if not required.

(15491) S. & Co. Ltd. W 14142/641. 90,000. 1/15. Forms C 2121/10.

Morduant

Routine Orders
by Colonel A. Sprot
Commandant No 1 Sect. L. of C.
September 30th 1915

No 68. Special.

The 5th Bn. The London Regiment (London Rifle Brigade) is leaving this Section shortly. The Battalion came from the front, where it had greatly distinguished itself, & it has since been employed on various & important duties on the Lines of Communications, often entailing much laborious work. These duties have always been performed with cheerfulness & zeal & the conduct of all ranks has been exceptionally good.

The Commandant heartily wishes all ranks of the Battalion every success in the

G.H.Q.

8th Bde 25.10.15

121/7551

Confidential

War Diary of

1/5th Battalion, City of London (Rifles)
(London Rifle Brigade)

from 1st October 1915 to 31st October 1915

Vol XII

Instructions regarding War Diaries and Intelligence Summaries are contained in F. S. Regs., Part II. and the Staff Manual respectively. Title pages will be prepared in manuscript.

WAR DIARY
or
~~INTELLIGENCE SUMMARY~~
(Erase heading not required.)

Army Form C. 2118.

Hour, Date, Place		Summary of Events and Information	Remarks and references to Appendices
October 1.	St OMER.	Guards, fatigues, + duties as usual. Orders to move to BLENDECQUES.	
2	"	Marched to BLENDECQUES, and billetted in village. Church parade.	
3	BLENDECQUES	Company training commenced.	
4		Company training, route marching and musketry to be done daily.	
5		Do. Capt. R.H. HUSEY rejoined Battn. from ENGLAND and took over duties of 2nd in command. Major THOMPSON took command of C. Co.	
6		Co. training, programmes to be submitted daily to I.G.C.	
7		Battn. route march 9 miles. General STOPFORD watched Battn. march by. Lieut. MAYNARD transferred to Railway Transport Establishment	
8		Company training.	
9		" Church parade.	
10		"	
11		"	
12		Battn. route march 13 miles. Dinners out.	
13		Company training.	
14		" Received warning that we were to leave GHQ area + relieve HAC. who are to be made into an O.T.C.	
15		"	
16		" Church parade.	
17		"	
18		" M.S. No. 610/2659 received, disallowing men to proceed home to take commissions in units serving at home.	
19.		Company training.	
20		Battn. route march 14 miles. Dinners out. Draft of 93 arrived from 3rd Battn. and were posted – : A Co. 20. B 22. C 30. D 20	
21		Company training.	
22		" Extract from LONDON GAZETTE 2nd Lieut G.G. BOSTON to be temp: Lieut:	
23		" Church parade.	
24.		"	
25		Battn. moved by motor bus to B RYFELD, and joined the 8th Brigade. 3rd Div. Battn. took over the billets of the H.A.C. Very wet weather, billets bad and very cramped. Received instructions from Brigade to organize Battn. Bombers and Snipers. Lieut: CHARLES appointed Intelligence + Sniping Officer. Lieut BOSTON + 2nd Lieut HILL bombing officers.	RHH. Capt.

1247 W 3299 200,000 (E) 8/14 J.B.C. & A. Forms/C. 2118/11.

Instructions regarding War Diaries and Intelligence Summaries are contained in F. S. Regs., Part II. and the Staff Manual respectively. Title pages will be prepared in manuscript.

WAR DIARY
or
~~INTELLIGENCE SUMMARY~~
(Erase heading not required.)

Army Form C. 2118.

Hour, Date, Place		Summary of Events and Information	Remarks and references to Appendices
October 26.	RYFELD.	Company training. Weekly programmes to be submitted to Brigade.	[signature] Capt.
27		"	
28		" ~~[illegible]~~ Informed that Battn. was to be trained as a Pioneer Battn.	
29		Pioneer training under RE instruction and Co. training. Leave recommenced.	
30		"	
31.		Company training.	
		During the month 17 NCOs men proceeded to England to take up commissions and 13 NCOs & men went to the Cadet School at BLENDECQUES, one of whom subsequently returned.	
		Extract from the LONDON GAZETTE 8th October 1915 —: The date of the appointment as temporary Lieutenants of the following is August 9th 1915 and not as stated in the Gazette of Sept. 18th 1915 —:	
		Lieut: A. B. WHITE	
		" F. H. CREWS.	
		" E. C. WILLS	
		" F. D. CHARLES.	
		" M. J. MAYNARD.	

1247 W 3299 200,000 (E) 8/14 J.B.C. & A. Forms/C. 2118/11.

W. P. Griffith & Sons Ltd., Printers, Old Bailey, E.C.
[481] W12130/2318 600m 2/15R 77 77 Forms C. 348 / 61

Army Form C. 348.

MEMORANDUM.

A189

From Staff Captain
No 1. Sect. L.O.C.
G.H.Q.

To
O.C.
L.R.B.

1/10 1915.

Ref. wire A.B. 9185 from I.G.C. re transfer of 5th Lond. R. to G.H.Q. Troops, I am directed to inform you that the battalion under your command will be transferred from L.O.C to G.H.Q. Troops from tomorrow 2nd inst.

S Preston
Staff Capt.

From

To

BO

ANSWER.

191 .

[illegible]

O.B. 206.

G.H.Q.T. 5876.

Second Army

==============

In view of the excellent material which exists in the battalion of the Honourable Artillery Company now with the 3rd Division, the Commander-in-Chief has decided to withdraw it to G.H.Q area and there use it as an O.T.C. Battalion.

It will be releived in the 3rd Division by the 5th London Regiment which is now undergoing a course of training in G.H.Q.area, and which will be ready to move forward about the 25th instant, on which date the Honourable Artillery Company should be ready to move to GH.Q.

It is desirable that the 5th London Regiment should be given further training before being put, as a unit, into the trench line.

General Headquarters. (sd) R. Wigham.

Major General,

14th October, 1915. Sub-Chief, General Staff.

H. & Sp., Ltd., Printers, Sylvan Grove, S.E.
[2540] W. 4555/2237 10,000m. 6/15

Forms C. 348 / 61

Army Form C. 348.

MEMORANDUM.

G.H.Q. TROOPS
No. 5816
Date. ...

From Adjt LRB	From H.Q. GHQ Troops
To H.Q. GHQ Troops.	To Adjutant L.R.B.
	ANSWER.
19. 10. 1915.	19/10/ 1915.
Would you please let me have a copy of the 2nd Army letter (you showed me on Friday last) relating to our future.	Herewith –
H. L. Johnston Capt & Adjt for O.C. L.R.B.	[signature] Staff Capt GHQ Troops

O.C.

London Rifle Brigade.

The battalion under your command will leave BLENDECQUES by bus at 9 a.m. on Monday 25th instant to join the 2nd Army - destination STEENVOORDE.

1 bus will be at your Headquarters at BLENDECQUES at 7.30 a.m. to convey billeting party in advance, and 34 busses at 8.30 a.m. to convey the remainder of the battalion, less transport section.

Rations for 25th will be carried.

The transport section will march from BLENDECQUES at 12 noon on 24th instant for HONDEGHEM. Route: ARQUES - RENESCURE - EBBLINGHEM - LES SIX RUES - STAPLE - LES CISEAUX. The Officer commanding the section will arrange with the Mayor of HONDEGHEM for billets for night of 24th - 25th. Orders as to forward march on 25th will be received from 5th Corps. Rations for 24th and 25th will be carried.

All billets at BLENDECQUES to be left perfectly clean, as they will be occupied the same day by an incoming battalion.

[signature]
STAFF CAPTAIN
G.H.Q. TROOPS

G.H.Q. for Brigade Major,

22/10/15. G.H.Q. Troops.

War Diary

8/31

1/5th London

Nov.

Vol XIII

121/7718

L

Confidential

WAR DIARY

of

1/5th CITY OF LONDON RIFLES

(LONDON RIFLE BRIGADE)

FROM 1st NOVEMBER 1915 TO 30th NOVEMBER 1915

Instructions regarding War Diaries and Intelligence Summaries are contained in F. S. Regs., Part II. and the Staff Manual respectively. Title pages will be prepared in manuscript.

WAR DIARY

or

~~INTELLIGENCE SUMMARY~~

(Erase heading not required.)

Army Form C. 2118.

Hour, Date, Place		Summary of Events and Information	Remarks and references to Appendices
1. November	RYFELD.	Pioneer and Company training. Capt SOMERS-SMITH rejoined from England and assumed command of A. Co. Colonel BATES proceeded to England on leave and Capt HUSEY assumed command of the Battalion.	[illegible] Capt.
2.		Pioneer and Company training	
3		do.	
4		do	
5.		do. Anniversary of arrival of Battn: in France. Concert held in STEENVOORDE.	M.S. No. 510/2659 cancelled
6		Final of Divisional Football Competition. Holiday granted to troops.	
7.		Company training. Church parade.	
8.		do. & Pioneer work. Captain OTTER reported to A.G. GHQ for duty with 1st Army HQ.	
9		do. " Captain SOMERS-SMITH takes over command of D. Co & Captain TREVELYAN A Co.	
10		do.	
11		do.	
12		do.	
13		do.	
14		Company training. Church parade. Pioneer training under RE. ceases.	
15.		Battn: route march 13 miles.	
16		Company training and Battalion drill.	
17		Brigade route march past General PLUMER commanding 2nd Army. One barn of B. Co HQ. billet destroyed by fire.	
18		Battalion inspected by General HALDANE commanding 3rd Division. Temporary Captain H.L. JOHNSTON appointed Adjutant of the Battn: with effect from 14th May 1915.	
19		Company training & gabion making	
20		" . Capt A.L. LINTOTT proceeded to ENGLAND ~~[illegible]~~ to join M.G. Corps at GRANTHAM.	
[illegible]		Capt J.R. SOMERS-SMITH took command of B Co from this date " A.T.B. de COLOGAN " " " D " "	

1247 W 3299 200,000 (E) 8/15 J.B.C. & A. Forms/C. 2118/11.

Instructions regarding War Diaries and Intelligence Summaries are contained in F. S. Regs., Part II. and the Staff Manual respectively. Title pages will be prepared in manuscript.

WAR DIARY

or

~~INTELLIGENCE SUMMARY.~~

(Erase heading not required.)

Army Form C. 2118.

Hour, Date, Place		Summary of Events and Information	Remarks and references to Appendices
RYFELD. November	21.	Gabion making and various fatigues preparatory to moving.	[signature] Capt.
	22	Cleaning up billets and various fatigues.	
	23.	Brigade moved to RENINGHELST and POPERINGHE. This Battn. marched to POPERINGHE via WINNEZEELE and WATOU. Distance 10½ miles. roads very bad and congested. Billetted in town. The Rev. K. N. CRISFORD attached to Battn.	
POPERINGHE	24.	Cleaning billets and various fatigues.	
	25.	Coy. route marches.	
	26.	The C.O. and Coy commanders inspected trenches at VOORMEZEELE where Battn. is to relieve LIVERPOOL SCOTTISH REGT. Coys. route marched.	
	27	Coy training. Adjutant visited trenches with M.G. officer.	
	28	" M.G. section and a proportion of Grenadiers, Snipers and telephonists relieved a similar number of men of the Liverpool Scottish.	
VOORMEZEELE.	29.	Battn. took over trenches at VOORMEZEELE, T 1, 2 & 3. R.5 and H.Q. dug-outs. Relief complete 8.55 p.m. One Coy remained in Camp under canvas at RENINGHELST, accomodation at VOORMEZEELE being insufficient. Battn. was to have been conveyed in Busses as far as RENINGHELST, but these were cancelled at the last moment, and Battn. had a long march to the trenches along very bad roads. Trenches very wet and in bad condition. 2nd ROYAL SCOTS on our right. 7th SHROPSHIRES on the left. Quiet but very wet night. <u>Casualty</u> 1 man slightly wounded by own Artillery.	
	30.	Worked on trenches. Slightly shelled. Wet night. Carrying and ration parties took 3-4 hours owing to terribly heavy going. <u>Casualty</u> 1 man severe head wound.	
December	1	Work on all trenches and building bomb proof shelters in village. Scout report received that enemy were mining 200 feet in front of R.3. 172nd Coy R.E. pushing out gallery towards them. Very wet night. <u>Casualty</u> 1 man slightly wounded.	
	2	Fine day, but wet night. Worked on trenches, put up wire and drained C.T. Had carrying party for material and working party from 8th E.YORKS. Enemy shelled ~~left~~ saphead leading to left crater. <u>Casualties</u> 2 men killed.	

(73989) W4141—463. 400,000. 9/14. H.&J.Ltd. Forms/C. 2118/10.

MOVE TO POPERINGHE

London Rifle Bde

Copy No. 5

8th. Brigade Orders. No. 15.

22nd. November 1915.

Reference 1/40,000 sheets 27 and 28.

1. The 8th. Brigade and attached troops will march to rest billets in RENINGHELST area and POPERINGHE to-morrow 23rd. inst.

2. 13th. Kings and London Rifle Brigade will march under Battalion arrangements to POPERINGHE. 13th. Kings to be clear of STEENVOORDE 10 a.m. London Rifle Brigade clear STEENVOORDE 10.30 a.m.

3. Starting point for 8th. Brigade less two Battalions-Road Junction, Sheet 27, Q.3.d. 6.3.

4. Route - see attached.

5. Order of March:-

	Units to pass Starting Point.	Billets. approx.
HdQrs, 8th. Inf. Bde.	9.45 a.m.	M.5.a. 6.10
2nd Royal Scots.	9.47 a.m.	M.4.b. 6.5
8th. East Yorks.	10.3 a.m.	M.4.b. 5.4
7th. K.S.L.I.	10.9 a.m.	M.4.b. 10.7
Cheshire Field Co. R.E.	10.15 a.m.	G.36.a. 7.4.
No. 8 Field Ambulance.	10.18 a.m.	BOESCHEPE.
No. 3. Coy. A.S.C.	11 a.m.	L.29.a. central.

Officers Commanding Infantry Units will detail an Officer to report at Starting Point 15 minutes before Unit is due to pass. Billeting parties of all 5 battalions - Strength 1 Officer, 3 other ranks per battalion will proceed with Staff Captain, 8th. Brigade by Motor Bus leaving Market Square at 8.30 a.m. 23rd. inst.

6.(a)1 Lorry will be at disposal of each Battalion for conveyance of blankets and fur coats. These lorries will be at STEENVOORDE bandstand at 9.30 a.m. Units will send a representative to meet their lorry and to conduct it to where the blankets and coats are stacked; they will also leave behind sufficient men to load the lorry. These lorries will make a second journey to fetch ~~xxxx~~

fetch timber and corrugated iron in possession of Units. Material of Battalions at POPERINGHE will be despatched on this journey to Brigade Headquarters at M.5.a. 6.10.

(b) A lorry will go round and call at all Battalion Headquarters to collect and return to Ordnance such stores that are to be handed in.7. Dinners on arrival at Billets.

8. Acknowledge.

Captain,

Brigade Major,

22/11/15. 8th. Infantry Brigade.

"A" Form. Army Form C. 2121.

MESSAGES AND SIGNALS. No. of Message

Prefix ... Code ... m.	Words	Charge	This message is on a/c of:	Recd. at ... m.
Office of Origin and Service Instructions. SECRET	Sent At ... m. To By		... Service. (Signature of "Franking Officer")	Date From By

TO { O.C. 5th London Rifle Brigade

Sender's Number.	Day of Month	In reply to Number	AAA
* BM 716	25		

Units will take over trenches 9th Bde at a later date as follows 13th Kings from 1/ Scots Fus ttt 2nd Royal Scots from 1/ Royal Fusiliers ttt London Rifle Brigade from Liverpool Scottish ttt 7th K.S.L.I. from 1/ Northumberland Fus ttt 8th East Yorks from 10th West Yorks ttt Addressed all units 8th Bde repeated 9th Brigade

From 8 Brigade
Place
Time 8 pm.

The above may be forwarded as now corrected. (Z) Captain Brigade Major

Censor. Signature of Addressor or person authorised to telegraph in his name.

* This line should be erased if not required.

(774-5) —McC. & Co. Ltd., London.— W 1789/1402. 150,000. 8/15. Forms C 2121/10.

SECRET.

Copy No....... 2

8th. INFANTRY BRIGADE ORDER NO. 17.

28th. November 1915.

Reference Sheet 28. 1/40000.

1. The 8th. Brigade will take over the front now held by the 9th. Brigade on night 29/30th.

13th. Kings L'Pool Regt. from 1st. Scots Fus. Trenches P.1. to P.4.

2nd. Royal Scots from 4th. Royal Fus. Trenches Q.2. to R.1.

London Rifle Brigade)
less 1 Company) from Liverpool Scottish. Trenches T.1. to T.3

7th. K.S.L.I. from 1st. Northumberland Fus. Trenches 23 to right of 76th. Bde. in 28.

8th. East Yorks will be held in Brigade Reserve at DICKEBUSCH.

2. The relief of Machine Guns, Grenadiers, snipers and a proportion of telephonists will be carried out on night 28/29th. under arrangements which have already been made by Specialist Officers concerned.

Motor busses rate 4 per battalion have been arranged to convey specialists 13th. Kings Liverpool Regt and London Rifle Brigade. Busses will be at POPERINGHE Station at 2 p.m. and reach H.29. b. cross roads at 4.15 p.m. where guides will meet them.

3. On 29th. inst. 8th. Brigade will march by Companies at 5 minutes interval, with Transport 5 minutes in rear of battalions from RENINGHELST via OUDERDOM H.14.c., H.15.d., H.22.b. to cross roads H.29.b. where guides will meet.

Starting Point G.34.d. 6.8.

1st. Company to pass Starting Point		Arrive H.29.b.
K.S.L.I.	2.30 p.m.	4.45. p.m.
London Rifle Brigade. (less 1 coy.)	3. p.m.	5.15. p.m.
Royal Scots.	3.30 p.m.	5.45. p.m.
13th. Kings. (By Bus from Poperinghe 4. p.m.)	4. p.m.	6.15. p.m.
East Yorks.	4.30 p.m.	6.45. p.m.

Boulbarick

Busses will be provided for London Rifle Brigade from POPERINGHE Station 2 p.m. as far as RENINGHELST.

4. 1 Company London Rifle Brigade on arrival at RENINGHELST will go into Camp, the position of which will be notified later

5. All Units in front line will take up water in tins to trenches.

6. No transport vehicles to re-cross YPRES - DICKEBUSCH road before 8 p.m.

7. R.E. Material for work on 30th. will be both indented for and taken up by 9th. Brigade.

8. O.C. Battalions will ensure that all ranks carry a spare pair of socks, and that feet are all treated with anti-frost bite or whale oil prior to starting for the trenches.

9. Gum boots will be taken over in the trenches.
A list of all trench stores taken over will be rendered to Bde Hd Qrs

10. Reports to 9th. Bde. Headquarters H. 29. b. 5.4.

G. T. B. Keith
Captain,
Brigade Major,
28/11/15. 8th. Infantry Brigade. 11 a.m

ROUTE.

Sheet. 27.	Road Junction	Q.3.d. 6.3.
	NONE BOSCH.	Q.4.c. 7.7.
		Q.10.b.
	GODEWAERSWELDE	Q.18.a. 6.7.
	Cross Roads	Q.12.d. 3.9.
	Level Crossing	Q.12.d. 8.7
		R.7.a.
	Road Junction	R.1.d. 3.5
	Road Junction	R.3.c. 9.1.
	BOESCHEPE	R.9.b. 8.3.
	Road Junction	R.9.d. 8.2.
		R.16.a.
	Cross Roads	R.18.a. 5.7.
Sheet 28.	Road Junction	M.19.b. 3.7.
	Cross Roads	M.13.d. 8.3
	Cross Roads	M.14.a. 5.10.
	WESTOUTRE	M.9.c. 3.8.
	HEKSKEN	M.3.c. 0.0.
	RENINGHELST	G.34.d. 2.8.

Index.........................

SUBJECT.

No.	Contents.	Date.
	5TH BATT'N, CITY of LONDON RIFLES.	
	WAR DIARY, DEC. 1915 (?)	

(56,425). Wt.24,741—161. 2000. 11/20. Gp.164. A.&E.W.

GHQ Infy

CONFIDENTIAL

WAR DIARY

of

1/5TH CITY OF LONDON RIFLES

(LONDON RIFLE BRIGADE)

from 1ST DECEMBER to 31ST DECEMBER 1916

Vol XIV

III Div

Army Form C. 2118.

Instructions regarding War Diaries and Intelligence Summaries are contained in F. S. Regs., Part II. and the Staff Manual respectively. Title pages will be prepared in manuscript.

WAR DIARY
or
~~INTELLIGENCE SUMMARY.~~

(Erase heading not required.)

Hour, Date, Place		Summary of Events and Information	Remarks and references to Appendices
VOORMEZEELE.	December 1.	Work on all trenches and building bomb proof shelters in village. Scout report that enemy were mining 200ft. in front of R.3. 172nd Coy RE. are pushing out gallery towards them. Very wet night. <u>Casualty</u> 1 man slightly wounded.	[signature] Major
	2	Fine day but wet night. Worked on trenches, put up wire entanglements in front of T.1, and started draining C.T. 8th E.YORKS supplied a working and a carrying party. Enemy shelled saphead leading to left crater; as a result 2 bombers posted there were killed	
	3	Wet day. Worked on trenches and draining. Trenches very bad indeed and parapet and parados continually fell in. 8th E.YORKS supplied working parties. Wet night. <u>Casualties</u> 1 man slightly wounded by shell fire. 1 man severely wounded by another man letting off his rifle while cleaning same: this man died in hospital same day.	
	4	Very wet day. BOOLAARBEK stream behind Battn. HQ. rose from 2'10" to 4'11" and partially flooded Reserve Co. dugouts. Trenches in shocking condition and rapidly deteriorating. Wet night. Carrying and working parties again greatly delayed. Slight shelling by enemy.	
	5.	Fine day but wet night. Stream fell to 2.10 again. Worked on trenches and draining generally. B.M. inspected line and strongly recommended concentrating on drainage. Specialists relieved by Liverpool Scottish. Relief not completed till 2.30 am. chiefly owing to the difficulty in carrying M.G. over the heavy ground. Trenches slightly shelled.	
	6.	Fine day but turned very wet at 3.45 pm. Battn relieved by Liverpool Scottish + 1 Coy. 4th R.F. Worked on trenches and carried up material for relief. Enemy shelled trenches slightly and C.T. during relief. 75 of the Battn. were conveyed to POPERINGHE in motor buses, remainder by armoured train from VLAMERTINGHE.	
POPERINGHE.	7	Resting and cleaning up generally.	
	8	Wet day. Route marching & musketry	
	9	" "	
	10	" "	
	11	" "	
	12	Weather moderate. Specialists relieved Liverpool Scottish as before in same trenches. Scottish report stream rose and flooded HQ dugouts twice.	

(73989) W4141—463. 400,000. 9/14. H.&J.Ltd. Forms/C. 2118/10.

Army Form C. 2118.

Instructions regarding War Diaries and Intelligence Summaries are contained in F. S. Regs., Part II. and the Staff Manual respectively. Title pages will be prepared in manuscript.

WAR DIARY
or
~~INTELLIGENCE SUMMARY.~~
(Erase heading not required.)

Hour, Date, Place		Summary of Events and Information	Remarks and references to Appendices
December. 13.	POPERINGHE	Fine day and night. Relief of Liverpool Scottish carried out quickly. Trenches still very wet and in a bad condition.	[signature]
14	VOORMEZEELE.	Fine day and night. Work on all trenches. R.E. assisted. Div. and Brig. commanders visited trenches. Casualties 2 men wounded.	
15.		Fine and cold. Work on all trenches. Commenced new M.G. emplacement. Front trenches relieved internally.	
16.		Fine day, wet night. Work on all trenches. Wired in front of T3. & T1&2. Our artillery bombarded enemy front line trenches and did a lot of damage.	
17.		Fine day. Work on all trenches. Again wired in front of T1&2 & 3. C.T. abandoned and decided to dig new one.	
18		Fine day. Work as usual. R.Scots reported new trench dug by Germans in front of R.3. This was bombarded by our trench howitzer, and during this part of R.Scots & T.1. trenches were evacuated. Germans made no reply. Casualties. 1 man killed	
19.		Fine night-day. Battn. stood to at 4.30 in consequence of German gas attack on Corps to the North. Our part quiet and no gas, but enemy fired a number of lachrymose shells down Ypres - Lille road which affected men in HQ dug-outs. More wire put out in front of trenches, & work as usual.	
20.		Fine day & night. Work as usual. New course for C.T. dug. Work as usual M.G. ~~staff~~ relieved by Royal Scots Fusiliers Casualties. 4 men wounded by shell at 'Whizz-bang' corner	
21.		Wet day. Work as usual. Battn. relieved by RSF. Relief complete at 8.12 pm. Battn. in detachments, marched ~~from~~ to VLAMERTINGHE and trained from there to POPERINGHE.	

(73989) W4141—463. 400,000. 9/14. H.&J.Ltd. Forms/C. 2118/10.

Instructions regarding War Diaries and Intelligence Summaries are contained in F. S. Regs., Part II. and the Staff Manual respectively. Title pages will be prepared in manuscript.

WAR DIARY
or
~~INTELLIGENCE SUMMARY~~
(Erase heading not required.)

Army Form C. 2118.

Hour, Date, Place	Summary of Events and Information	Remarks and references to Appendices
POPERINGHE. December 22	Companies at the disposal of O.C. Corps for training &c.	[illegible]
23	"	
24	"	
25		
26	Church parade	
27	M.G. section and 5 officers relieved RSF in same trenches as before.	
28	Cleaned up billets. Battn. relieved ROYAL SCOT FUSILIERS in same trenches as before, being conveyed by armoured train to VLAMERTINGHE.	
29.	Fine day. T1+2 shelled by 8" shells and about 25 yds of trench blown in. This was completely repaired during the ~~day~~ night. Casualties 3 men wounded, ~~[illegible] Sgt Shaw subsequently died~~	
30.	Fine day, wind in gas quarter, so Battn. stood to. R.5 and VOORMEZEELE shelled. Work on all trenches continued and wiring party strengthened wire. Detailed reconnaissance of trenches carried out and ~~[illegible]~~ trench map commenced. Casualties. 5 men wounded.	
31	Fine day. Wind still in gas quarter. Battn. still standing to. Quiet day, but as New Year came in a good deal of artillery fire and rifle fire was indulged in. Work on all trenches as before.	
	—	
	Extract from LONDON GAZETTE 15th December. Capt. R H HUSEY to be Temp Major to date from 16 April 1915.	

1247 W 3299 200,000 (E) 8/14 J.B.C. & A. Forms/C. 2118/11.

London Rifle Bde

SECRET. Copy No. 5.

8th. INFANTRY BRIGADE ORDER NO.13.

1. The 8th. Infantry Brigade will be relieved by 9th. Infantry Brigade on night 6th/7th. Decr. and move into the rest camps at RENINGHELST and billets at POPERINGHE as occupied before.

Battalions will be relieved as follows:-

7th. Kings Shropshire L.I. by 1st. Northumberland Fus.
London Rifle Brigade by Liverpool Scottish.
2nd. Royal Scots by 1st. Royal Scots Fus.
13th. Kings Liverpool Regt. by 12th. West Yorks Regt.
8th. East Yorks Regt by 4th. Royal Fus.

One company 4th. Royal Fus. will move into VOORMEZEELE.

2. Machine Gun Sections with guns and a proportion of Bombers and snipers and 2 signallers of the Battalions in the front line will be relieved on night 5th/6th. and all front line bombing posts will be taken over. The actual number of specialists will be telephoned to Battalions to-day.

Guides will be provided as follows:-
For N. Fus at 4.30 p.m. at CAFE BELGE cross roads H.29.B.
For R.Fus.Gun at 4.40 p.m. " " " " "
For W.Yorks at 5. p.m. " " " " "
For R.S. Fus. at 5.10 p.m. " " " " "
For Liv.Scots at 5.20 p.m. " " " " "

Two busses for conveyance of 13th. Kings and London R.Bde. specialists will be at cross roads H.18.d.

3. Guides will be detailed to meet incoming battalions on 6th. inst. as follows:-

UNIT.	No. of Guides	Rendezvous.	Time	Remarks
K.S.L.I.	3.	CAFE BELGE H.29.b.	4.15 p.m.	
E.Yorks	1.	do.	4.40 p.m.	To conduct ½ coy 4th. R.Fus. to KINGSWAY.
13th. Kings	3.	do.	4.45 p.m.	
2nd.R.Scots	3.	do.	5.15 p.m.	
L.R.Bde.	3.	do.	5.45 p.m.	
2nd.R.Scots	2.	do.	6 p.m.	To conduct 1 coy 4th. R. Fus to VOORMEZEELE.

8th. East Yorks will be prepared to move on relief at 3 p.m.

4. All Battalions will select their own route for returning and march

march independently.

[5)] Motor busses will be placed at disposal of Battalions at N.16.D. cross roads.

13th. Kings.......8 busses.
L.R. Bde..........8 busses.
2nd.R.Scots.......2 busses.
7th. K.S.L.I......2 busses.

[6)] Inventories of stores to be handed over to relieving Units. [7)] O.C. Battalions in trenches will command until relief is complete and notify same at once [By wire] to Bde. H.Q.

[signature]

Capt,

Brigade Major,

5/12/15. 8th. Infantry Brigade.

8th Brigade.

3rd Division.

WAR DIARY

Battalion went to 56th Division (169thBde)
5th February 1916.

1/5th BATTALION

LONDON REGIMENT

JANUARY 1 9 1 6

5th London Regt

Jan

Vol XV

To 169 Bde 5/2/1916.

3rd Div.

/-

8 Inf.

1247 W 3299 200,000 (E) 8/1. J.B.C. & A. Forms/C. 2118/11.

Instructions regarding War Diaries and Intelligence Summaries are contained in F. S. Regs., Part II. and the Staff Manual respectively. Title pages will be prepared in manuscript.

WAR DIARY

or

~~INTELLIGENCE SUMMARY~~

(Erase heading not required.)

Army Form C. 2118.

Hour, Date, Place		Summary of Events and Information	Remarks and references to Appendices
VOORMEZEELE	1916 1 January.	Fine day. Work on all trenches in spite of memo from G.O.C. Div: that the day was to be observed as a holiday as much as possible. Quiet on both sides.	[signature] Major
	2.	Wet day. Work as usual. Trench mortar put 1 shot into enemy trench opposite right crater. BOLLAARDBEEKE rising, mark 2'0". Casualties 1 man wounded. Rfn. HAMMOND D. killed.	
	3.	Fine day and night. Work as usual. More wire put out. Stream rose to 3'3" then began to fall. Casualties Rfn. RIVERS F.B. killed.	
	4.	Fine day and night. Work as usual in trenches, assisted by 56th Coy R.E. Battn: relieved by R.S.F., relief complete at 9.5 p.m. Battn: marched to DICKEBUSCH and billetted there, being attached to 9th Brigade for all purposes. Casualties 1 man wounded.	
DICKEBUSCH	5	Resting	
	6	On fatigue work in trenches at night	
	7	"	
	8	" Casualties Rfn. PRICE D.A. killed.	
	9	No fatigues. Specialists relieved R.S.F. in same trenches as before.	
VOORMEZEELE	10	Battn: relieved R.S.F. as before. Relief complete 8.16 p.m., fine night. New Co. H.Q. erected in T.3.	
	11	Fine day and night. Work on all trenches and wiring party put up more wire.	
	12	" " " " more wire put up.	
	13	" " " " . Patrol found enemy erecting	
	14.	breastwork between craters.	
	15.	Fine day and night. Two officer patrols our front, but nothing much discovered, but brought in luminous peg and one or two "souvenirs". Orders received that we are to link up two bombing posts in the craters. Ground reconnoitred.	
	16	Fine day and night. Work as usual, but orders given by G.S.O.1 to erect at least 4 more traverses in T1 & 2. These were commenced. Casualties 3 men wounded.	
	17	Fine day & night. All men available worked on traverses. M.G. section relieved. Casualties 1 man wounded.	

1247 W 3299 200,000 (E) 8/14 J.B.C. & A. Forms/C. 2118/11.

Army Form C. 2118.

Instructions regarding War Diaries and Intelligence Summaries are contained in F. S. Regs., Part II. and the Staff Manual respectively. Title pages will be prepared in manuscript.

WAR DIARY
or
~~INTELLIGENCE SUMMARY~~
(Erase heading not required.)

Hour, Date, Place		Summary of Events and Information	Remarks and references to Appendices
VOORMEZEELE	1916 18 January.	Showery. The 4 traverses completed in T22, and work as usual on all trenches. Battn: relieved by RSF and relief complete at 7.55 pm. Battn: marched to RENINGHELST and went into tents.	[signature] Major
RENINGHELST.	19.	Co inspections of kit etc and bathing.	
	20	Battn: programme of training carried out. fine weather.	
	21	" " "	
	22	" " "	
	23	" but not continued in view of having to supply two fatigue parties, one working	
	24	at the BLUFF & 1 at DICKEBUSCH LAKE. Casualties 2nd Lieut WHEATLEY wounded.	
	25	" Lewis guns section relieved RSF in same trenches as before.	
		Battn marched to VOORMEZEELE and relieved RSF in trenches as before.	
VOORMEZEELE	26.	Fine day. Trenches very wet indeed and worse than ever before. Work on draining and building parados. Enemy exploded small mine in front of right crater. no damage done. Casualties. 4 men wounded.	
	27.	Battn: took over U23 B with 1 officer 31 OR and 4 grenadiers. No wire in front. Slightly shelled. Worked on traverses, and drainage. 2 M.Gs in front of Tr 22 fired a lot at night.	
	28.	Fine day & night. 2 M.Gs definitely located. 45th Batty: registered on them and when they opened fire again our guns shut them up. Work as before.	
	29.	Very fine but foggy. Brigadier instructed us to concentrate entirely on making approach to left crater post safe by day — connecting right & left crater posts & drainage. Work as usual. Abnormally quiet and very few enemy flares fired. Very good reconnaissance carried out by 2nd Lieut POGOSE, who cut some enemy wire	
	30	Very foggy and misty which stopped all sniping and gun fire. Wind went S.E. so Battn. stood to. Good work done on all trenches. Secret instructions received that all firing was to be stopped. This commenced at 4.15 pm. — Cancelled 10.45 pm. Major HUSEY took over command of Battn. while Col. BATES was on leave.	
	31.	Fine but misty. Received armour piercing bullets — these very efficacious. Enemy very quiet indeed. Specialists relieved by RSF. Received official notification that Battn was leaving the Div. shortly. Good work done on draining and approach to bombing post.	

1247 W 3299 200,000 (E) 8/14 J.B.C. & A. Forms/C. 2118/11.

Instructions regarding War Diaries and Intelligence Summaries are contained in F. S. Regs., Part II. and the Staff Manual respectively. Title pages will be prepared in manuscript.

~~WAR DIARY~~
or
~~INTELLIGENCE~~ SUMMARY.
(Erase heading not required.)

Place	Date	Hour	Summary of Events and Information	Remarks and references to Appendices
1916 January			During the month the following officers joined the Batty: from the 3rd line unit —	[illegible] Major R.B.
			Lieut TITLEY P.	
			2nd " POCOCK. B.L.E	
			" CLODE-BAKER G.E.	
			" CAMDEN F.M.	
			" BROMILEY B.	
			" WHEATLEY F.M.	
			" PULLEN L.H.	
			" POOL E.E.	
			WILLIAMSON E.R.	
			HEWITT F.E.	
			SELL C.H.	
			SMITH. H.	
			A Brigade M.G. section was formed on the 18th Jan: to which we had to send our 4 guns and crews and limbers and drivers.	
			A protest was entered at the time stating that as these men were in the T.F. and should not be transferred — this protest was subsequently re-entered on the Batty leaving the Div: Lieuts: PULLEN & POOL were the M.G. officers attached.	
			Captain ROBINSON & Lieuts: BARKER & HOGG returned to ENGLAND in exchange for 3 officers from the 3rd line unit.	
			Extract from LONDON GAZETTE 19 January 1916.	
			Temp: Lieut: WALLIS F.H. to be temp. Captain 18/1/16	

1577 Wt. W10791/1773 500,000 1/15 D. D. & L. A.D.S.S./Forms/C. 2118.

www.ingramcontent.com/pod-product-compliance
Lightning Source LLC
Chambersburg PA
CBHW081411160426
43193CB00013B/2152